JUDGMENT AT BRIDGE

By
Mike Lawrence

Published by
Devyn Press, Inc.
Louisville, Kentucky

FIRST PRINTING MAY 1976
SECOND PRINTING   OCTOBER 1982
THIRD PRINTING   OCTOBER 1983
FOURTH PRINTING   JANUARY 1985
FIFTH PRINTING   APRIL 1986
SIXTH PRINTING NOVEMBER 1987
SEVENTH PRINTING   SEPTEMBER 1989
EIGHTH PRINTING   JULY 1990
NINTH PRINTING AUGUST 1992
TENTH PRINTING   APRIL 1995
ELEVENTH PRINTING   NOVEMBER 1997
TWELFTH PRINTING   APRIL 2000
THIRTEENTH PRINTING   APRIL 2008

Printed in the United States of America.

Published by
Devyn Press, Inc.
3600 Chamberlain Lane, Suite 206
Louisville, KY   40241
1-800-274-2221

ISBN 0-910791-81-3

TABLE OF CONTENTS

Chapter One — The Opening Bid
  Common Errors of the Opening Bidder   1
  The Econo Club   6
  Welcome to Diamonds   12
  One Notrump   21
Chapter Two — Overbidding and Underbidding
  Unconscious Overbidding   25
  The Modern Approach in Competitive Auctions   31
  Responding to Takeout Doubles   32
    The One Notrump Response   37
    Free Bids   52
Chapter Three — The Takeout Double   58
Chapter Four — Difficult Hands   67
Chapter Five — Preference,
  Or the Fine Art of Letting Partner Play the Hand   71
  Judgment Situations   75
Chapter Six — More Double Trouble
  Bidding After Opponents' Takeout Double   85
Chapter Seven — The Fine Art of Judgment   103
Chapter Eight — Defense   118
  Play to Third Hand at Notrump   119
Chapter Nine — Suit Preference — The Art of Confusion   127
  Standard Situations   134
  Signals in Non-Mandatory Situations   142
  Suit Preferences During the Middle of the Hand   148

Books by Mike Lawrence

HOW TO READ YOUR OPPONENTS' CARDS
Prentice Hall — 1973

WINNING BACKGAMMON
Pinnacle — 1975

JUDGMENT AT BRIDGE
Max Hardy — 1976

THE COMPLETE BOOK ON OVERCALLS IN CONTRACT BRIDGE
Max Hardy — 1980

TRUE BRIDGE HUMOR
Max Hardy — 1980

THE COMPLETE BOOK ON BALANCING IN CONTRACT BRIDGE
Max Hardy — 1981

PLAY A SWISS TEAM OF FOUR WITH MIKE LAWRENCE
Max Hardy — 1982

DYNAMIC DEFENSE
Devyn Press — 1982

MAJOR SUIT RAISES
Texas Bridge Supplies — 1982

THE COMPLETE BOOK ON HAND EVALUATION IN CONTRACT BRIDGE
Max Hardy — 1983

PLAY BRIDGE WITH MIKE LAWRENCE
Devyn Press — 1984

FALSE CARDS
Devyn Press — 1986

CARD COMBINATIONS
Devyn Press – 1986

SCRABBLE
Bantam Press — 1987

MIKE LAWRENCE'S WORKBOOK ON THE TWO OVER ONE SYSTEM
Max Hardy — 1987

PASSED HAND BIDDING
Lawrence & Leong – 1989

BIDDING, QUIZZES, THE UNCONTESTED AUCTION
Lawrence & Leong — 1991

THE COMPLETE GUIDE TO CONTESTED AUCTIONS
Lawrence & Leong — 1992

TOPICS ON BRIDGE
Mike Lawrence — 1991

INTRODUCTION

Every year, millions of men and women, mostly quite young learn how to go through the motions of playing bridge. They expect to play bridge once or twice a month as a change from watching television or going to a movie. They do not expect to become experts, and in fact they don't.

Heaven bless the millions of beginners, for without them there would be no such thing as my daily newspaper columns.

Every year, also, a few dozen experienced bridge players, likewise mostly quite young become experts. They would like to play bridge every day and every night, and in fact some of them do.

They have no need of blessings from Heaven or any other source. Give them cards, opponents, and perhaps a tournament director, and they will count the world well lost.

In between the beginners and the experts are the millions of men and women, mostly middle-aged, who enjoy playing bridge once or twice a week but find many other activities enjoyable. They know they would enjoy bridge more keenly if they understood it a bit better — still, however, as just one of their many leisure pursuits.

It is to these intermediate players that Mike Lawrence addresses his excellent books. Anybody who has read his first work, "How to Read Your Opponent's Cards," will address himself to this book and will not be disappointed. It continues the job of helping the intermediate player become a better intermediate player. (Do not look for a book to help you become an expert. There are books that will take you from beginner to advanced intermediate, but the final transition to expertdom comes about from playing, talking, and living bridge with other monomaniacs during every waking hour of many months, sometimes many years. This is not written in scorn: supremacy in *any* field is the product of talent applied to the point of monomania.)

"Judgment," says the old joke, "comes from experience, and experience comes from making mistakes. Therefore judgment comes from making mistakes."

The most common mistake, Mike Lawrence points out, consists in thinking that a bid means what you want it to mean at the moment rather than what your partner will surely understand it to mean. Judgment can begin only when you get over being Humpty Dumpty.

Mike Lawrence doesn't discuss all of the common mistakes in this excellent attempt to improve your bridge judgment. What he does is point out the *direction* in which you should think. If you need a reminder a year or two from now, let us hope that another excellent book by Lawrence will be ready to give you pleasure and help.

I'll be waiting for it, too.

Alfred Sheinwold

Beverly Hills, California
May, 1976

PREFACE

Many years ago when I first became interested in the world of bridge, a question would arise. Discussion with the players of the moment would occasionally provide an answer. But mostly it produced an argument. Inevitably, in search of a final solution the more debatable questions were submitted to an expert for final arbitration. (Is there such a thing as an undebatable question in bridge?)

At least it was our intent to submit the questions to an expert. Unfortunately, the expert was not always around when we needed him and the problem would either be forgotten or relegated to the "let's ask later" file. But by the time we managed to find ourselves in a position to ask an authority those "let's ask later" questions, we found the questions had been mislaid or we had so many as to swamp the poor soul.

Fortunately, however, we were always able, when necessary, to go to one of the various learned texts on bridge. You know the type. *How to Play Bridge in 1,000 Easy Lessons.* Or *Everything You Always Wanted to Know About Bridge, But Had No One to Ask.*

And surely you have had something like this happen. You and your partner have just gone for 1,100 in a competitive auction. And the opponents of course could have made nothing. There followed the usual emotional outbursts and someone, probably your partner, said something like this:

"Your bid guarantees ten points." To which you replied: "No way I need 10 points! If I had a good hand I'da done this or I'da done that" . . . etc . . . etc.

Your opponents sat there quietly for a while, perhaps enjoying the discussion. Or were they enjoying the 1,100? In any case, bridge players being what they are, and a bridge problem being what it is, soon you and your partner were not doing all the arguing. Hardly. Your right-hand opponent was busy arguing with you and your left-hand opponent was busy arguing with your partner. This of course led to a free-for-all during which nothing was learned or gained except for a wet table top and a soggy deck of cards, the result of someone's drink being caught up in the melee.

Ultimately, one of the cooler heads among you remembered having read thus and such in one of the aforementioned volumes and someone was able to produce the book in question.

A small bet was made and one of you began wading through the book in search of an answer. Inasmuch as you had been doubled in a competitive auction, you looked first under "Doubles" where you found:

Negative Doubles
Responsive Doubles
Takeout Doubles
Lead-Directing Doubles
Penalty Doubles
Invitational Doubles

None of these seemed to fit your problem.

So you looked next under "Competitive Bidding" where you found:
Overcalls
Weak Jump Overcalls
Overcalls at the one level
Overcalls at the two level
Overcalls after a weak two bid
Bidding after a preempt
Raising partner after an overcall
Free Bids
Bidding after a double
And nowhere was there a hand like the one under discussion.

But the person who had claimed to know that the answer would be found in this book persevered . . . (Was he the one who suggested the bet?) and sure enough, there it was. Not where you would expect it, perhaps, but there nevertheless. Perhaps it was found in the section on "Problems of the Responder" or perhaps it was under "Rebids by the Opener." The only thing you knew for sure was that the discussion contained in the text did not do justice to your problem.

Here then is the purpose and intent of this book.

Any book attempting to teach bridge must, in order to do so completely, discuss thousands of possible situations. This means that many very important and common areas of bridge are given only passing mention. All this in order to make room for many vague, obscure, and unlikely situations which may appear once in a lifetime. For instance, when is the last time your partner bid 4NT, asking for aces, and your right hand opponent bid 5S?

Recently I have taught a large number of intermediate and advanced bridge players. These lessons have always included a substantial number of hands to be bid and played. In the process of giving these lessons it became clear that certain areas of bridge were consistently misunderstood. Other areas were obviously well learned and no problems were evident. (This material was not what I taught in my lessons, but was what the student already knew — or did not know, as the case occasionally was.) Nor did it follow that the lack of understanding meant the topic was necessarily difficult.

It is then my intention to discuss those areas of bridge which I feel have been poorly or insufficiently discussed in the past. These are divided into bidding and defense, with numerous questions and detailed answers. Throughout, there is emphasis on "judgment" as a concept. Too much of bridge cannot be defined by points or other criteria. Hopefully, a multitude of examples and questions will help make up for this lack of definition.

The reason there is no section on play is that there are already sufficient excellent texts covering that aspect of bridge. Defense and bidding, on the other hand, require certain partnership rapport. It is the common misunderstandings between partners which I hope to identify and correct.

FORMAT — HOW TO USE THIS BOOK

The format of the book follows this general pattern. An area of bidding (or play) is set forth. I discuss it in general terms and then examine the various kinds of errors that frequently occur. Looking at these errors and comparing what did happen with what should have happened will hopefully help in understanding what went wrong.

Following each discussion is a quiz, with answers immediately following. After all, at the bridge table you do not have to bid or play two hands at once, so why do so in a book?

Notice that throughout, emphasis is put on *WHY* and emphasis is put on *JUDGMENT.* If both of these concepts are understood, then something has been learned and not merely acquired by rote.

In some of the areas I discuss there exists a "modern" approach quite different from the more "standard" approach which I emphasize. When this occurs I examine the "modern" approach as well. No effort is made to evaluate one approach against the other. That is something you will have to decide for yourself. The only thing in this area that I would strongly recommend is for you and your partner to be playing the same system. When two people are playing together, but using two different systems, the ensuing disasters can often assume legendary proportions. It is of such misunderstandings that newspaper column hands are made.

Bear in mind that the topics selected here are those which have proven to be unclear to some number of players. For some people, much of this will have substantial meaning, and I hope for them that a few misconceptions can be eliminated. For others, most of this material will present few or no problems. For the latter this should serve as a review. Perhaps there are areas of partnership disagreement which could be resolved.

CHAPTER I   THE OPENING BID

Common Errors of the Opening Bidder

For the most part, the opening bid does not tend to present any problems. However, there are a few areas of confusion and vagueness which I consider to be the result of poor generally accepted bidding practices.

What suit would you open holding the following hands?

♠ AQ1087   One spade. Open the higher of two five-card suits.
♥ KJ942
♦ Q3
♣ 2

♠ 108764   One spade. Same reason as above.
♥ AJ973
♦ K7
♣ A

♠ K7   One heart. Same reason. Open the higher of two
♥ J8642   five-card suits. The relative quality of the
♦ AKQ108   suits should not affect the opening bid.
♣ A

Does it seem strange that there would be a question on any of these three hands? One would not think so. But in one of my advanced classes I have this hand:

♠ Q10764
♥ AKJ104
♦ KJ
♣ A

According to the rule, the opening bid should be one spade. For some reason though, the opening bid was occasionally one heart. Whenever this occurred, I would ask a few questions of the opening bidder as well as of the partner of the opening bidder. The following two-way conversation is typical of this hand.

"Why did you open with one heart?"

"I have a very good hand and my hearts are better than my spades."

"What are you going to bid if your partner responds, for instance, with one notrump?"

"I would bid two spades."

"What will this tell your partner?"

"It will tell my partner that I have a very good hand."

"What will your partner know about your distribution?"

At this stage of the conversation, the opening bidder is usually ready to resign and his answer to the last question is either "I guess I should have opened with one spade" or the answer is an even more resigned "Oh."

1

Depending on the trend of this conversation I would at some point switch to the partner of the opening bidder with the following discussion.

"If you should respond with one notrump to your partner's one heart bid, and your partner then rebids two spades, what do you think he has?"

"At least 16 or 17 points."

"And what is his distribution?"

"Probably four spades and five hearts. Maybe five spades."

"If he has five spades, why didn't he bid them first, instead of one heart?"

"I guess because he has more hearts than spades."

"Is there any chance partner does not have more hearts than spades? Can he have five of each?"

"No."

Almost every time I have this discussion, the opening bidder sounds slightly unsure of himself as the conversation proceeds. However, the partner, in answer to my questions, replies quickly, confidently, and correctly. Why?

The first thought one might have is that the partner of the opening bidder was guided by the conversation between me and the opener. I feel, however, the reason for this discrepancy is the result of what you might call "table pressure." It is not at all the same thing to make a decision, as did the opening bidder, as it is to discuss it abstractly, as the responder did.

It was clear to me that the players involved in the above situation were good players. I was quite confident they knew the correct bid. I was also sure they knew the correct reasons for that bid. There was just some undefinable something that kept these people from doing what they really knew was right. It may result from that "table pressure" I have already mentioned. I saw it happen to a large number of players. I have no doubt it occurs with many more.

I cannot give any suggestions as to how one avoids this psychological hazard, but perhaps the realization that it exists may be of help. If so, then this rather lengthy look at "what suit should I open" may have provided some benefits. Certainly the problem, if it exists, of table pressure does not limit itself to just opening bids as we will see later.

One other specific problem of the opening bid is this one:

♠ 7	If your system allows four card major suits,
♥ KQ87	then you might consider bidding one heart.
♦ AJ42	Otherwise you will have to choose between one
♣ K1097	diamond and one club.

I do not intend to get involved in the merits of five card major openings as opposed to four card major suit openings. What I am interested in are the other considerations involved here.

If, for the sake of this problem, you do desire to open with a minor suit, which one will it be? And while you are deciding, ask yourself this question: "What is my partner over there going to be most likely to bid?"

Well, if your partner should find a one heart response, it would be beautiful and you would be happy to raise hearts. But you and I both know that partners are not all that cooperative. In the real world partners always manage to do the wrong thing. Almost certainly your partner is going to bid one spade.

Now what difference could that expected one spade bid make to your choice of opening bids? Consider what you would rebid over the one spade bid if your opening call had been one club. So? Would you rebid one notrump? How many spades would you expect your partner to have if he opened with one club and then rebid one notrump after one spade by you? Would you not expect him to have two, or even possibly three spades? He should have them just as you should.

If, instead of a one notrump rebid, you chose two hearts or two diamonds:

You	Partner		You	Partner
1♣	1♠		1♣	1♠
2♦		or	2♥	

will there be any objections to your having bid the hand this way?

♠ 7
♥ KQ87
♦ AJ42
♣ K1097

Ask your partner what he thinks you should have to do that. Ask him "How many points does this bidding show:

1♣ — 1♠ — 2♥ ?"

He will say you need about sixteen or more. He will tell you that you have made a "reverse" bid which guarantees about an ace more than a minimum opening hand.

Do you think this hand is worth more than a minimum opening bid? Do you think it is worth an ace more? If you think so, you are entitled to lifetime membership to the optimist's club. Dues are free but you still have to pay when you go for 1400.

If you think this hand is a normal minimum, you will not want to rebid two diamonds or two hearts. You and your partner will be in agreement as to the meaning of the bids.

Do you still wish to open with one club, or would you prefer one diamond? If you do bid one diamond, can you envision having trouble later in the auction? If partner bids one heart, you can still raise. But if he bids one spade, as expected, will you be able to rebid without all the aggravations there were when you started with one club?

You	Partner
1♦	1♠
?	

Here, the rebid of one notrump has the same objections as before. Likewise, so does a rebid of two hearts. You need a better hand. But if you opened with one diamond, you can rebid two clubs easily and comfortably should partner find that anticipated one spade response.

Is there no objection at all to bidding this hand in that fashion? There is one possible drawback, but it is minor. Only if partner puts you back in two diamonds will you be in any danger.

You	Partner
1♦	1♠
2♣	2♦

And even in this case there is no guarantee that two diamonds will not be a good contract. It may well be the best spot. And if you began by opening with one club, you will not be likely to find your diamond fit at all; or if you do find it, you may end up too high.

Quiz
What do you open with:

♠ 87
♥ AQ1087
♦ 9
♣ KQ876

One heart. The higher of two five-card suits.

♠ KJ987
♥ A2
♦ 7
♣ AQ1096

One spade. Some people advocate bidding one club when holding five spades and five clubs. They may be right. This is the only combination of two five-card suits which may violate the usual rule. Other than this the rule must be: Open the bidding in the higher ranking of two five-card suits. Incidentally, the people who open these hands with one club are not really that confident that they are right. You and your partner should decide. Then stick to your decision.

♠ 98642
♥ AQJ107
♦ AQ
♣ 8

One spade. Follow the rule. Repetitious? Perhaps. But one spade is the correct bid both here in the quiz and at the table, notwithstanding the number of people I have *seen* open this with one heart.

In the next part of the quiz you will not have quite the same considerations as in the first part. In selecting your opening bid, you will have to decide: 1) What suit shall I open? 2) What will my rebid be? You will find that the answer to the second question will often influence your answer to the first question. This planning ahead is known as the principle of anticipation or "preparedness."

But no matter what you call it, it is nothing more than looking ahead a bit in the bidding and planning what you will do in such and such case. Surely it is better to take a few seconds now in deciding your correct opening bid, than to agonize later over what may be a selection of bids ranging from bad to worse to impossible.

♠ 8
♥ AQ107
♦ QJ97
♣ A862

If you play that four card majors may be used, you might open one heart. If you play that you need five cards to open one heart or one spade, you will open one diamond or one club. Your choice?

Referring to the material earlier, your choice should be one diamond. This is in anticipation of partner's possible responses. His most likely bid of one spade can be handled with no embarrassment. You will rebid two clubs.

♠ 42
♥ 97
♦ AKQ8
♣ K8764

Here, the principle of being prepared works quite well for you. If you open one club, then over partner's response of one heart or one spade you will be poorly placed. You will not want to rebid one notrump

because of the small doubleton in the other major suit. Nor do you want to rebid two clubs on such a poor suit. You cannot bid two diamonds, as that promises a much better hand. On the other hand, if you open one diamond, then you can rebid two clubs without misdescribing your hand or your values.

♠ 7
♥ K1076
♦ KQ109
♣ AKJ8

Well? For a change you have got a good hand rather than one of those doggy minimums. Does this make any difference to you in your choice of bids? For the purposes of this question, choose only between one

club and one diamond. If you like, one heart is acceptable, but ignore it for the moment. You will find that the usual objections to the one club are still here, with one exception. Now you have the strength to open one club and rebid two diamonds. Can you find any objection to bidding in this fashion? There is an objection and it can be summed up in the following rule.

RULE: When you open the bidding and then rebid in the next higher suit, your first suit is always longer than the second.

You	Partner	
1♣	1♥	You have more clubs than diamonds.
2♦		

You	Partner	
1♦	1♠	You have more diamonds than hearts.
2♥		

Both of these auctions are "reverses" and guarantee hands worth at least an ace more than a minimum. In addition, both auctions describe hands in which the suit opened is the longest.

The opening bid with the quiz hand should be one diamond, intending to rebid two clubs. Of course if partner bids hearts, you would be delighted to raise.

The Econo-Club

The next area of opening bids is the much maligned one club. So far in this discussion, all of the problems have been concerned with "what suit should be opened" when you really did have a choice. However, some hands do not present clear-cut choices, even though they have full values for an opening bid.

One would think that if some number of hands containing difficult choices of opening bids were presented to a large number of players, there might be a fair number of selected bids. Such is not the case. What usually happens is that when no easy bid is available, reason is set aside. It is as if there were a computer program in the minds of some players. The program runs like this.

(1)   Do you have an opening bid?

(1A) If yes, do you have a five card or longer suit?

(1Aa) If yes, open it.

(1B) If no, can you open with one notrump?

(1Ba) If yes, do it.

(1C) If you have no five card suit, and you cannot bid one notrump, bid one club.

The result of all this seems to be a "club fever" or "club mania," the main symptom of which is a lemming-like idolatry of the "econo-club." The things I have seen done in the name of the "econo-club" are quite staggering, to say the least. My own experience suggests there is a major area of misunderstanding here. It is further reinforced by a large number of letters I handled when I was running a bridge answering service. Out of a thousand letters, more than a hundred were about the short club. The ways in which it was misused were astounding.

Here are a few of the multitude of hands I have seen opened with one club. Some of them admittedly do not have clear-cut answers. But on the other hand, there are a number which are quite remarkable. As you look at these hands decide what, if not one club, you would bid.

♠ 8742
♥ AKQ10
♦ K104
♣ Q5

If playing four card majors, bid one heart, otherwise one diamond. Always open your longer minor when choosing between them in a hand like this.

RULE: Never bid one club or one diamond without at least three of them.

♠ K72
♥ AQ108
♦ K1084
♣ J3

Again, either one heart or one diamond.

♠ A2
♥ KQ7
♦ J8742
♣ K108

One diamond. No reason for anything else.

♠ 97642
♥ KQ
♦ AJ
♣ A874

One spade. What else? If you start with one club, you can never get across to partner that you have five spades and four clubs.

♠ AJ87
♥ KQ97
♦ 8742
♣ K

This seems like anything except one club. The reason the person did bid a club was "I play five card majors, and the diamonds were not biddable!"

♠ AKJ98
♥ K103
♦ 4
♣ AKJ4

This seems like a normal one spade. But the hand was opened one club in order "to keep the bidding low for partner."

♠ A1087
♥ KQJ9
♦ AKQ7
♣ J
descriptive start.

Hard to believe, but this was also opened with one club because "I can support anything partner bids." Certainly true, but what if partner raises clubs? Any of the other three suits looks like a more

♠ K107
♥ AQJ8
♦ AK104
♣ 103

This looks like a one notrump bid, having the required 16 to 18 points with the correct distribution. The person holding this, though, began with the usual one club giving the reason, "I can't open with one notrump because I don't have clubs stopped." I did not believe it either.

Later I will express some ideas about when you should or should not open with one notrump on some unclear hands. This is taken up in a section by itself.

♠ Q103
♥ KJ7
♦ KQ105
♣ K42

Again, one diamond is correct. Not one club. This particular hand type is the one most often opened with a misguided Econo-club. Remember this hand. It comes up again in the ensuing discussion.

The previous nine hands were all examples of the misusage of the one club opening bid. In all cases the hand did not include a club suit but yet one club was the chosen call. Why?

A look at these hands suggests three possible reasons. The first reason seems to stem from a reluctance to open in a bad five card suit. This sort of thing happens.

North

♠ A72
♥ J3
♦ K874
♣ J862

South

♠ 98653
♥ K104
♦ A2
♣ KQ4

With South the dealer, the bidding proceeds busily: one club, pass, one notrump, all pass. The defense leads a diamond, or perhaps a heart, and declarer goes down one or two. Nothing abnormal happens, but declarer just does not have enough tricks. Unlucky? Perhaps.

At this stage North has usually noticed that two or three spades could have been made. What happens now is that North says to South something like this.

"Why didn't you bid spades? You have five of them!"

To which South replies, "They were very bad spades."

North: "So why didn't you bid two spades over one notrump? I would have passed you there."

South was ready to say something about a reverse, but the East player who dealt the next hand opened the bidding with a pass, and South found himself staring at his yet unarranged, untouched pile of thirteen new cards. Picking them up as quickly as possible, fully aware of the glares of the three other players who had already arranged their hands, South hastily sorts the suits and finds himself looking at something like this:

North

♠ A72
♥ J3
♦ K874
♣ J862

(North's hand repeated for convenience)

South

♠ K1083
♥ Q
♦ A6
♣ AK10953

The auction goes almost as before. South bids one club, and North responds with one notrump. South, thinking about his speech on reverses — the one he did not get to give — tries two spades. North, true to his word says "Pass!" and that is that. Five clubs of course is quite cold. When in fact the spades divide five and one, two spades is down a few and the partnership is in less than perfect harmony.

This time South is quick to point out that clubs is far better than spades and why didn't North raise clubs, etc., etc. North has momentarily forgotten the previous hand and can only agree that clubs is better.

Inevitably, things proceed until something like this occurs. Perhaps it occurs the same day. Perhaps it occurs a week later. But you can be sure it will occur and you can be sure the feelings of irresolution will carry over to this occasion. South picks up another familiar hand:

South

♠ 109764
♥ AK7
♦ K10
♣ A42

Forgetting for a moment the results of the previous hands, he opens again with one club. Partner of course finds that one notrump call and South, now becoming distantly aware of past problems, begins to cogitate. The first instinct to pass, the path chosen formerly, is momentarily pushed aside by the thought that two spades might be a far superior contract. South remembers that two spades is in fact a reverse, but hasn't partner promised to pass a rebid of two spades? In fact partner *did* pass two spades on an earlier hand. So South tries two spades. This of course gets around to North who has finally gotten the idea that the two spade bid shows a good hand with more clubs than spades. Pleased with his new understanding, North corrects to three clubs and smiles at South to let him know that they are finally getting the system down pat.

This however does not at all please South who is sadly reconsidering his two spade bid. Surely, thinks he, it would have been better to play in one notrump than in three clubs. And with this thought I would agree one hundred percent.

But wouldn't it be easier to open with one spade? Then you could play in one notrump when it was right and in two spades when it was right. It would no longer be necessary for either player to have to make a correct guess, let alone both players.

Things like this really do happen and the result of these unusual bids cannot help but upset the partnership rapport.

The second common misuse of one club is on a big hand in which "I don't want the bidding to be passed out." Or "I wanted to make it easy for partner to bid." This problem is easy to deal with. Ask yourself this question, given the following hand: Would you rather be passed out in one spade or in one club?

♠ AKQ107
♥ 4
♦ KQ10
♣ AJ42

Even if partner does respond to your Econo-club bid, how will you ever convince him you have five spades and only four clubs? All the problems that were apparent in the previous discussion will be even more so here.

9

And there may be some additional problems as well! With weak opening hands such as:

♠ 107642
♥ KQ7
♦ AJ
♣ K103

a one club bid could easily lead you to the wrong partscore, and *perhaps* the wrong game. But opening one club with:

♠ AKQ107
♥ 4
♦ KQ10
♣ AJ42

is *very* likely to get you to the wrong game and it would be no surprise to find someone reaching a terrible slam as well.

Here are a couple of hands and how they were bid. What was wrong with their bidding is clear enough. But what would you have done instead?

North
♠ J742
♥ Q83
♦ KJ86
♣ 42

South
♠ A3
♥ KJ1097
♦ A107
♣ AQ3

These hands, with South the dealer were bid:

South	West	North	East
1♣	Pass	1♠	Pass
2♥	Pass	2NT	Pass
3NT	All Pass		

With North the declarer, a club lead through the AQ3 was enough to set the contract. Unlucky? Certainly it was not impossible to make three notrump, but there were two things wrong with the final contract. The first thing wrong was that the wrong hand was declarer. The strong South hand would have had a much better chance of making three notrump. The second thing wrong was that four hearts declared by South would be most unlikely to fail. Is there any way to reach four hearts? The obvious way is to bid, for instance:

South	North
1♥	2♥
4♥	

Easy? Yes. Effective? Yes. So why try something else which so often leads to confusion at best and disaster at worst?

The third kind of club bid which is the source of so many bad results looks like this:

♠ AQ107	♠ KJ86	♠ AK7
♥ KQ96	♥ AK74	♥ KQ94
♦ Q42	♦ 7642	♦ 7654
♣ 76	♣ Q	♣ Q3

What do these hands have in common? The first thing that strikes the eye is that the club suit is completely nonexistent. The second thing is that there is no five card suit available. This group of hands is usually of the balanced variety with the exception of a 4-4-4-1 distribution.

Many of these hands can be easily handled if you play four card majors. If your system permits, then you can open a spade on

♠ AQ107		♠ KJ86
♥ KQ96	or	♥ AK74
♦ Q42		♦ 7642
♣ 76		♣ Q

and one heart on

♠ AK7
♥ KQ94
♦ 7654
♣ Q3

But many people insist on having five card majors and in this case the hands must be opened with a club or a diamond. Even those people who do not object to opening four card majors may occasionally decide to open with a minor suit. The usual reason in this case is that the major suit or suits are too poor to open. Something like these:

♠ Q642	♠ A432
♥ Q986	♥ KQJ
♦ AQ10	♦ Q42
♣ K2	♣ Q108

Only the most rabid major suit bidder would dream of bidding a spade on either of these. So given that you are going to choose between clubs and diamonds, which one will it be?

"Welcome To Diamonds"

Meet the most maligned suit in bridge. Diamonds. They look like this: ♦ . They are not too aesthetic to look at. Sort of like squares trying to pull themselves together but not quite making it. But they work hard at it as evidenced by their red complexion.

Diamonds are a most unappreciated suit. They just are not recognized. So . . . I would like to propose the following rule, which should forever put an end to many silly and easily avoidable disasters.

RULE: With balanced hands on which you decide not to bid a major suit, bid the *longer* of your minor suits. If both minor suits are three cards only, open one club.

Now on some hands you will have four of each minor. One club will probably be acceptable, but you should keep in mind the earlier discussion on rebidding problems.

Quiz

Bearing the rule in mind, what will you open with each of these hands? If you feel like opening one heart or one spade on some of these hands, then answer instead this question: If someone *made* you open with a minor suit, which one would it be?

♠ K1087 One diamond. I know one heart looks most reasonable,
♥ AKQ8   but for this quiz the rule is bid your longest minor.
♦ J98
♣ J2

♠ J876   One club. With three of each, open with one club.
♥ AK7
♦ KQ7
♣ J54

♠ A43   Again, one club. Even though the diamonds are so
♥ K765   much better. If you should decide to fudge a bit
♦ AK5   and try one diamond, I do not imagine much bad would
♣ 1087   happen.

♠ 7   One diamond. Do not forget to plan ahead. Over one
♥ K965   spade you will be able to rebid two clubs easily and
♦ AQ104 accurately.
♣ AJ65

♠ A765   One diamond. Do not let the poor quality of the
♥ K54   diamond suit persuade you to bid one club instead.
♦ J765   J765 is better to open than AQ.
♣ AQ

♠ K42   One diamond. Same reason.
♥ A1065
♦ 5432
♣ AQ

♠ K765   One diamond. This one may be a bit harder, but it
♥ AJ42   is still correct. Open your longer minor suit.
♦ 765
♣ KQ

Before proceeding to reasons for this rule of opening the longer minor, answer a few more questions, after which it will be possible to get to the heart of the matter. Describe what your partner should have for each of the following auctions. Is partner's bid weak or strong?

Partner   You   You have shown a hand with four or more
  1♣   2♣   clubs and from six to nine points in high
  2NT   cards. Partner's 2NT bid is asking you
to do one of three things.

(1) Pass if you have a balanced minimum for your 2♣ bid.

♠ J72
♥ 42
♦ Q1076
♣ K1084

(2) Bid three clubs if you have a distributional minimum.

♠ 42
♥ 82
♦ Q432
♣ K9876

(3) Bid three notrump if you have a maximum raise for your 2♣ bid.

♠ 42
♥ Q3
♦ K765
♣ A9642

As you can see, your partner says he wants to be in game if you have eight or nine points. Therefore he must have seventeen or so himself. His 2NT bid is not weak, it is strong and is highly invitational. Partner may have:

♠ AQ82
♥ KQJ2
♦ K4
♣ K54

If you play 16 to 18 point notrump openers, you would probably not have opened one club. But if your one notrump bid shows 15 to 17 points, then this hand would be what partner should have for the auction:

> 1♣   2♣
> 2NT

The auction   1♦   2♦
>   2♠

is also a strong sequence. And it is forcing. It is known as a "game try." Partner would like to know if you have a maximum or a minimum, and if possible he would like to know where your cards are. After this auction, you would respond as follows.

♠ 4   Three diamonds. Just a minimum with nothing extra.
♥ 976
♦ Q8765
♣ K1064

♠ 92   Two notrump. Something in both unbid suits, but not
♥ K107   too much.
♦ 98742
♣ KJ3

♠ 92   Three notrump. A good maximum with both unbid suits
♥ KJ3   stopped.
♦ Q864
♣ K1083

♠ 42   Three clubs. I have a maximum, but I cannot bid
♥ 86   notrump because I am worried about hearts.
♦ QJ876
♣ AJ42

♠ 4   Three diamonds. With a minimum you cannot afford to
♥ 72   bid three clubs. It would sound like a better hand.
♦ 98642
♣ AJ432

And what does partner's hand look like to be asking all these questions?

> 1♦   2♦
> 2♠

Well, he has one of two kinds of hands. First, he has some kind of balanced hand and is hoping for three notrump. He might have:

♠ AK2   ♠ AKQ
♥ 42   ♥ 42
♦ KQJ109   ♦ AKQJ109
♣ AJ3   ♣ 52

The second possibility is that he has a good distributional hand and needs only some specific cards from you to make a game.

♠ AQ76
♥ J
♦ AKJ976
♣ Q2

If you could bid three notrump over two spades he would be happy. And if you bid (say) three clubs then he would be delighted to bid five diamonds.

♠ AQ2
♥ A10
♦ AKJ986
♣ 42

If the bidding went similarly in this situation then he could bid three notrump, knowing all suits were secure and the needed tricks would be available.

Now for some players the above is already well understood, and for some it may be new. In any event, it may help to clear up areas of partnership disagreement.

Why was so much time devoted to simple auctions such as these?

1♣   2♣   1♦   2♦
2NT   2♠

The reason was to emphasize that these rebids by the opening bidder were strong! They are looking for better things: They are not attempts to escape from the minor suit. The opening bidder is asking:

Do we have a game?
Can we make a slam?
Is a partscore the best we have?
Partner, what do you think?

Notice this one difference between the two auctions:

1♣   2♣   is invitational, but *not* forcing.
2NT

1♣   2♣   is also invitational, but *is* forcing.
2♥

Finally, it is possible to get a look at what happens when players abuse the Econo-club. You have already seen what happens when you have neglected to open with your best suit when you were lucky enough to have one:

♠ 108764
♥ AQ2
♦ K4
♣ AJ7

Now see what happens when the "cure-all" magic of the Econo-club is brought to use on balanced or semi-balanced hands.

What went wrong in the following chamber of horrors?

North

♠ Q3   South opened one club. Perhaps it was unfortunate
♥ J64   that North passed. Or was it fate?
♦ Q9876
♣ 542

South

♠ AKJ2   I really do not know how to get to six diamonds
♥ A865   on these cards. But I do know how to get to diamonds.
♦ AK104   Bid them. If South opens one diamond then some
♣ Q   reasonable contract will be reached.

Some of the people who have had such disasters have informed me that the cause of this one was not in the opening bid, but in the failure of partner to respond to one club.

"Do you play one club openings as forcing?" I inquired.

"No," was the prompt and exceedingly firm response.

"What then would you bid over partner's one club bid holding:

♠ Q3
♥ 62
♦ 987652
♣ 862

or is this a hand with which you would pass partner's opening one club bid?

"I would bid one diamond," was the answer.

Perhaps one should respond one diamond to one club with this hand. Certainly you should if partner has:

♠ AKJ2
♥ A865
♦ AK104
♣ Q

Because then you can make six diamonds and probably not make one club. But what if partner's hand happens to be:

(1) ♠ A92 (2) ♠ AJ76
♥ KJ8   ♥ A
♦ Q3   ♦ K2
♣ AKQ54   ♣ AQ9754

In the first case he is going to jump to two or three notrump and he is going to go down. In the second case he is going to jump shift to two spades and you will have to do one of two things:

(1) Pass the jump shift, which will ruin the partnership confidence, or

(2) Keep on bidding, out of respect to the jump shift, in which case you will get too high and you will go down again, also doing little for the partnership confidence.

Silly? Yes. And it could be avoided simply by opening the bidding normally and by responding normally.

If you and your partner want to take up a "one club forcing" system, fine. It will probably work out O.K. But there is no place for an "It's not forcing but we never pass" one club. It is a wonderful system for result merchants, swamis, and the like; and quite inefficient in the hands of mortals. It just does not work.

Let us get back to the more common of the deviations and their subsequent and predictable consequences.

North
♠ 542
♥ 76
♦ QJ76   South bid one club, and North raised to two clubs.
♣ KJ107   South did not care for this too much and made an effort
South   to escape from a trap of his own doing. He bid two
♠ AKJ7   spades, hoping North would pass. But, as was just
♥ J542   shown, the two spade bid shows strength and is forcing.
♦ K76   North properly interpreted the bid and returned to
♣ Q2   three clubs. This was not exactly what South wanted to
hear and he made one last effort to escape from clubs. He bid three notrump.

Well, escape from clubs he did, but the result otherwise left a bit to be desired. Three notrump was not a success. In fact it was down three.

Note the correct bidding. South bids one diamond (the longer of two minor suits) and North raises to two diamonds. South then passes! Perhaps you would prefer to be in one notrump. So would I. But certainly two diamonds is a better contract than three notrump.

On the other side of the coin, this sort of thing occasionally happens.

North
♠ J72
♥ 943
♦ Q7
♣ K9864
South
♠ AKQ3
♥ 2
♦ K96
♣ AQJ53

South starts with one club and North raises to two clubs. South envisions a game (slam) and tries two spades. North then passes, and again, a less than ideal contract is reached. Why? It seems that North thought South was trying to escape from clubs. Two spades happened to make an overtrick, but as five clubs was a lock, South felt obliged to express a few opinions.

How do you feel these hands should be bid? Would you just jump to five clubs after partner's raise? Here, admittedly, that would work quite nicely. But what if partner over there has a different hand? Instead of having:

North
♠ J72
♥ 943
♦ Q7
♣ K9864

he might have either of these hands:

Your hand	North	North
♠ AKQ3	(1) ♠ 72	(2) ♠ J2
♥ 2	♥ KQ9	♥ 1087
♦ K96	♦ 10542	♦ A42
♣ AQJ53	♣ K1083	♣ K8642

In the first case the correct contract is three notrump, and in the second case six clubs is going to make. The only way to bid these hands to the correct contract is to be able to bid two spades after a raise to two clubs, and this will work only if the partnership is aware of what the two spade bid means.

With responding hand #1, the bidding might be:

South	North
1♣	2♣
2♠	2NT
3NT	Pass

With responding hand #2, the bidding could go similarly or exactly like any of these sample auctions:

South	North	South	North	South	North
1♣	2♣	1♣	2♣	1♣	2♣
2♠	3♦	2♠	4♣	2♠	4♣
4NT	5♦	5♣		4NT	5♦
6♣				6♣	
(a)		(b)		(c)	

Even if you do not get to slam, it must surely be better to get to a good game contract which makes rather than play in a partscore or the wrong game contract going down.

Here is another altogether too common situation. It is like a two-part comedy. If it seems familiar it should be.

Part I:

North
♠ 762
♥ 9
♦ Q10764
♣ A1087

The bidding begins:

South	North
1♣	2♣
?	

South
♠ KQ83
♥ A1076
♦ KJ2
♣ 93

The further details of this auction can remain undiscussed. The final contract is almost never going to be satisfactory. Whatever it is, it will almost certainly go down doubled. Perhaps down quite a few doubled. Whatever happens will leave food for thought in the minds of both players. Usually nothing is ever done to improve the situation, and whenever someone opens with one club there is a nagging fear in the atmosphere, which brings us up to . . . . . .

Part II:

North
♠ 762
♥ 9
♦ Q10764
♣ A1087
South
♠ K4
♥ Q87
♦ AJ2
♣ KJ654

This time the auction begins:

South	North
1♣ (1)	1♦ (2)
1NT (3)	? (4)

(1) Why not? Normal enough.
(2) Remembering the previous hand.
(3) Why not again. Perfectly OK.
(4) Well. Last chance to guess how many clubs partner has. Or is it right to rebid the diamonds?

Clearly, if your partner opens one club on random hands then your chance of making the correct guess here is equally random. One notrump here went down three. It turns out that four clubs could be made if declarer finds the queen of clubs. In any case, the hand would have produced at least nine tricks at clubs, which is only five more than were taken in the actual contract of one notrump. Is this bridge?

It is hard to imagine this sort of thing happening. But it does. And it will again. Only when the various liberties taken in the name of the Econo-club have ceased, along with the other less common aberrations, will these and related mishaps no longer haunt the game.

In the first part of this book the question of what to open was "What suit should I bid?" However, there is another group of hands which fall into the category of "Should I open in a suit at all?"

If you decide to open in a suit, then you go back to the "which one" question. But if not, then you open with one notrump.

This then is the next area of discussion.

It will be very short.

And it will probably be controversial.

Certainly it will not have the approval of very many teachers. For in fact, what I intend to recommend is directly contrary to what is published in most leading texts on bidding, but I am convinced that what I am going to suggest is clearly right, at least in the long run. So all other opinions aside for the moment, here goes. **RULE: If your hand contains the correct number of points to open one notrump, do it except when it is clearly right to open something else.**

What makes it right to open something else?

The answer to this is found in the same principle of anticipation that was discussed earlier. The best way to demonstrate this is to give a number of hands with appropriate discussion. Both sides of the problem are considered, i.e., textbook approaches and textbook reasons, as against my approach with my reasons.

For the purposes of these hands assume the one notrump range is 16 to 18 high card points.

♠ KQ7 A typical one notrump. Everyone
♥ A1086 will agree with this.
♦ J96
♣ AK7

♠ AQ872 One spade. Very seldom should you
♥ K42 open one notrump with a five card
♦ 972 major suit.
♣ AK

♠ J8762 One notrump. This is in keeping with the
♥ AJ idea that you should open one no-
♦ KQ9 trump unless you have a clear other
♣ KQ10 choice. Bidding one spade would
certainly not be wrong but one
notrump should be preferred. Note that when you have a five card major suit, you have all the other suits stopped for sure. You should not have an unstopped suit when you open one notrump on a hand containing a five card heart or spade suit. Most players will open this hand with one spade. But they can't object too strenuously to bidding one notrump.

♠ 872	One heart. Here you have an
♥ Q10874	unstopped suit, spades.
♦ AQ	
♣ AKJ	

♠ 92	One notrump. This won't be a pop-
♥ AJ97	ular choice among teachers. BUT . . .
♦ KQ10	There is no other clear choice of
♣ AK86	bids. Some people will tell you
	to open one club. Sure. That's

very nice, but these people never tell you what to bid when partner
responds one spade. If you rebid one notrump, you'll probably make it. But
you are going to miss a lot of good game contracts. Partner is going to think
you have 13 to 15 points and here you are with seventeen.

Likewise, if you rebid two notrump, partner will think you have 19 or 20
HCP. You don't have that either. It's still only 17.

Nor is the hand worth a reverse bid of two hearts should you get a one
spade response to your opening one club bid. So in spite of what all the
textbooks say, there cannot be any reasonable bid other than one notrump.

Please don't take all of this to mean that opening one notrump with a small
doubleton in one suit is always going to be right, or even safe for that matter.
No. What I am saying is that IN THE LONG RUN, THERE WILL BE FAR
FEWER PROBLEMS FROM OPENING ONE NOTRUMP THAN FROM
OPENING ONE OF A SUIT.

Having a completely unstopped suit is never a reason (by itself) for not
opening one notrump. If the principle of anticipation suggests future
problems, ignore the unstopped suit. After all, when you bid one notrump,
you have told your partner so much about your hand that the following
bidding is usually quite easy. Hopefully this will compensate for the
occasional poor result. I think it does.

♠ Q109	One notrump. Don't let the small doubleton
♥ 76	stop you. Remember, if
♦ AKQ10	the hand is otherwise suitable, one
♣ AJ94	notrump will be OK. In any case,
	here you do not have another clear

cut bid. Certainly you don't have another bid which is guaranteed to
produce no later complications.

♠ 987	Here you have a rather extreme
♥ 974	example. The bid should be one
♦ AKJ	notrump, in spite of the fact that
♣ AKQ10	you have two unstopped suits. If
	you open one club, you will be

very lucky if you don't run into trouble with your rebid. Opening one
notrump has good chances of working out all right.

By opening one notrump, you are hoping to make your bidding easier in
the long run. I give no guarantees on any particular hand.

♠ AQ107   In the previous hand, you had two
♥ 872   unstopped suits, yet one notrump
♦ 93   was chosen because of rebidding
♣ AKQJ   problems. Here you again have
                 two unstopped suits, but you
should begin with one club because the bidding will present no problems.
Whatever partner should bid, you will have an easy call. If he bids one heart
or one diamond, you will bid one spade. This is an easy rebid. If partner's
response is one notrump, you will pass or raise notrump. It would depend on
what partner showed by his one notrump bid. If he shows six to nine, you
pass. If he shows nine to eleven, you raise to two notrump.

♠ A1073   One notrump. You have the same
♥ Q82   high cards and the same distrib-
♦ K3   ution as before, but with all suits
♣ AQJ9   stopped the correct bid is the
                 highly descriptive one notrump.
Bid one notrump unless you have reasons not to.

♠ 82   One notrump. You would prefer
♥ AQ109   something else. If you play that four
♦ 1076   card majors are allowed, then one
♣ AKQJ   heart could be best. But one notrump
                 is going to be superior to a one club
opening often enough to be significant.

♠ K7   One notrump: A five card minor is
♥ AKJ   in no way a deterrent in deciding
♦ KQ7   to open with one notrump.
♣ J8762

♠ Q3   Again one notrump. True, you do
♥ K97   have a nice club suit, but you
♦ QJ7   have no good rebid if partner bids
♣ AKJ97   one diamond or one heart or one
                 spade. Whatever rebid you choose,
you will find serious flaws.

♠ K2   One notrump. Even six card minor
♥ KJ9   suits may on occasion be included
♦ AQ   in one notrump openings.
♣ KJ7642

♠ 43   One club. Not all six card suits are suitable for
♥ A2   opening one notrump. Here you have an
♦ K43   excellent suit. A club slam or game may be
♣ AKQ10765   possible. The reasons you could open the
                 previous hand one notrump were:

1) All suits were stopped

2) The suit was not too good

Basically, I believe the standard rules for opening one notrump are too restrictive. They are nice when they work, but a strict adherence to them just leads to more serious problems of a frequently unsolvable nature.

Putting this material in summary form, we have:

1) Open one notrump when you have no clear alternative.

2) Avoid having five card major suits when you open one notrump. If you do have five hearts or five spades, then you must have all suits stopped.

3) Unstopped suits are not a serious restriction against opening one notrump. Of course you would rather not have a small doubleton, but by opening one notrump you may be able to avoid later serious problems.

4) With strength concentrated in two suits, try to open the bidding in a suit if you can see no problem in rebidding. Otherwise, open one notrump.

5) Some hands may include a six card minor suit, but if this is the case, then all other suits must be stopped.

I repeat again that whether you follow the discipline in the textbooks, or the carte blanche approach suggested here, you will have problems. I believe only that by using this laissez faire style the sum of your problems, and therefore the sum of your poor results, will be measurably less than before. Besides, you will get to play more hands.

CHAPTER II OVERBIDDING AND UNDERBIDDING

Do you know any overbidders? Are there any in your favorite foursome? Who are they? Your opponents perhaps, or maybe your partner, or even, heaven forbid, you? No? Not even one? This I surely doubt. In fact experience has suggested to me that on the average, any given table of bridge will include at least four overbidders.

At least? Yes, at least. One must not overlook the ubiquitous kibitzer. This person, more than any other, combines that rare sense of overbidding and underbidding — as required — which guides him to the double-dummy contract in each hand. One would expect no less of a kibitzer than perfection.

Seriously though, and forgetting the kibitzer, I suggest that all four players may be overbidders. They are, but not in the normal meaning of the word.

Overbidding usually means something like jumping to game when a simple raise would have been enough; or bidding a slam at the merest hint; or perhaps overcalling on what might be less than normally considered sufficient. These overbids and their obvious relatives are well known to all bridge players. And if you want to tell me that you never overbid, at least in light of the above, then I will not argue with you.

But there are a number of hand families in which overbids are regularly, even routinely, made. And what is worse is the fact that most of the players making these overbids do not even know it.

When, in fact, they suffer a setback, perhaps only a partscore going down, maybe a game that should have been a partscore, or even a more alarming disaster such as down 1400, the bad result is attributed not to overbidding, but to bad luck.

This is not an area where rules will have much meaning, as the situations do not have that much in common.

Instead, the concept of what I term "unconscious overbidding," or UO, will best be approached by examination of many separate situations.

The first of these UOs I intend to discuss is also one of the most common. It has various forms, but it usually comes up looking a bit like this.

Let us pretend that you and I have just cut each other for partners in a rubber bridge game on a commuter train. Since time is short, we dismiss our conventions with the following brisk repartee.

"Standard bidding, partner?"

"To be sure. Who dealt?"

It turns out that you did, and on the first hand you opened with one spade. I raised to two spades, and after some thought, you went to three spades.

At this point, the attractive girl on your left (your secretary, I believe, the one I have been hoping to meet) asked you what the three spade bid was all about.

You replied that my bid of two spades showed about six to ten points. You had around eighteen and wanted to be in game if I had the maximum for my raise. We were in clear agreement as to this meaning, and as I had a rather poor hand, the bidding stopped. Even three spades was not safe, but with a little careful play, it was made.

Our opponents, both of whom I knew from times past, were quite reasonable players. At the completion of the hand, (how they managed to wait eludes me) they turned to the kibitzer and as one voice began —

"Dummy had only six points, so that was not enough to bid to game. If dummy had had another king, giving him a maximum hand for the raise, then he would have gone on to four spades."

Now whether they are trying to teach points to, or score points with, the secretary, I have not the foggiest idea. But I do know they understood what the auction was all about.

Shortly thereafter, the player on my left opened with one spade. The player to my right raised to two spades. I had a reasonable hand with six good hearts, so entered into the bidding with three hearts. The opening bidder rebid three spades, and after you passed, the responder raised to four spades. He showed his hand to the kibitzer and said:

"See, this hand is worth almost ten points, so I'm going to bid a game. We should have no problems making it."

When four spades was passed around to you, I remember you looked a bit confused when you doubled. And the dummy looked a bit confused when declarer went down three tricks. The dummy also looked a bit embarrassed, but I suspect that was because the kibitzer was beginning to ask questions.

"What happened?"

Well, it was a bit unlucky to go down three. Declarer could always have gone down just two, or perhaps even just one, but when he tried to make the contract — disaster. There was just no way to make four spades.

"What happened?"

Now if you knew that the cards did not divide unreasonably, nor did the trumps break badly in that four spades contract, could you tell me what happened?

What happened here was merely one more in a long and heretofore unceasing chain of UOs. This time a disaster occurred. Usually the result is not this serious. Sometimes the UO goes unpunished completely. Usually, at least, it goes unnoticed.

Have you worked it out yet?

I am going to show you one hand from the preceding debacle.

It is the only hand that matters.

It is the declarer's hand.

It was:

♠ Q10974
♥ K2
♦ AJ73
♣ Q4

Now you may not think that's a three spade bid when the bidding goes:

1♠	Pass	2♠	3♥
?			

You may feel that this person got just what he deserved.

You may feel like skipping the rest of this chapter because you would never *never* make a bid like that, and why should you be bothered to read about it?

Wait.

I agree. It was a bad bid. I agree it shouldn't happen. But it does. Admittedly, the price here was stiff, but anyone who often does this sort of thing must expect this sort of result.

Avoidable? For sure.

But I have seen this particular UO over, and over, and over, and over. Good players make it. Average players make it. And poor players make it.

Auctions like these:

1♠	Pass	2♠	3♣
3♠			

or

1♥	1♠	2♥	2♠
3♥			

or

1♠	2♣	2♠	3♣
3♠			

For some reason which I honestly can't understand, it just keeps happening. A player opens the bidding and his partner raises. Somewhere along the line (refer to the sample auctions) the opponents compete a bit. And when this happens, the opening bidder always competes to the three level, regardless of his hand.

And this is wrong, wrong, wrong.*

Look at this auction.

1♠	2♠
3♠	

It shows a good hand. It shows around eighteen points.

Now look at this auction:

1♠	Pass	2♠	3♥
3♠			

And this one:

1♠	2♦	2♠	3♦
3♠			

They also show good hands. "Partner, do you have a maximum or a minimum? Do you think we have a game?"

Unfortunately, some people feel they have to confirm that they did in fact open the bidding and no one is going to push them around.

* For the moment remember this is standard bidding. A look at modern techniques later.

If you had opened this hand,

♠ Q10974
♥ K2
♦ AJ73
♣ Q4

would you wish to confirm it? Neither would I, but it happens all the time.

A fast look at the mathematics of this. If you have the above hand, and the bidding goes:

1♠   Pass   2♠   3♥
3♠

one of two things will happen:

1) Your partner will have a minimum hand and he will pass.

And you will go down.

2) Your partner will have a maximum hand and he will go to game, expecting you to have a better hand. Do you think you can make a game? Neither do I. Down again. And on occasion, down doubled, and down many.

Now if instead you say pass, one of two things will happen:

1) Partner will have a minimum and he will pass. Some of the time you get a plus result anyway — when you can set three hearts. You could not have gotten a plus result had you bid.

2) Partner will have a maximum hand for his raise and he will bid three spades if his hand is suitable or he may even be able to double three hearts.

Isn't this much better? When you can't make three spades, you won't be bidding it and going down. And when you can make three spades you will be able to play in three spades making, rather than four spades going down. Not only will your results be better, but the partnership confidence will improve. For when you stop making the kind of error just described, you will avoid not only bad results of overbidding but an occasional worse result of underbidding.

This kind of thing happens. Another two scene act.

PART ONE:

Responder

♠ Q87   You and partner have had the usual
♥ J82   UO sequence which went:
♦ AQ42   1♠   Pass   2♠   3♥
♣ J63   3♠   Pass   4♠   All pass

Opener   No one doubled, but the contract
♠ A10652   was down two and there was no way
♥ K3   for the opponents to make three hearts.
♦ K963
♣ K8

28

Responder

♠ 1076
♥ K2
♦ KJ732
♣ 1042

Opener

♠ AJ843
♥ AJ3
♦ 10
♣ Q963

Undaunted, you tried again. Much as before, the auction went,

1♠	Pass	2♠	3♥
3♠	DBL.	All Pass	

Again, down two, and again you could have defeated three hearts. Now if this sort of thing continues, it could get expensive. Even when no one doubles.

While you cogitate over the manner and means of losing points in part one, consider now the new ways to incur bad results.

PART TWO:

Responder

♠ J72
♥ Q97
♦ K7652
♣ 83

Opener

♠ A10843
♥ K82
♦ AQ
♣ A93

This should seem familiar. You bid with partner in the following fashion,

1♠	Pass	2♠	3♥
?			

Your first thought was to bid three spades, hoping partner would bid game with a maximum. But realizing the sort of trash you've had for this bidding on earlier hands, you tried a direct bid of four spades. Would you believe it? Down again. Unlucky. Partner had the wrong hand.

Responder

♠ KJ2
♥ 94
♦ KJ1073
♣ J105

Opener

♠ A10843
♥ K82
♦ AQ
♣ A93

And now the ultimate in aggravation. North and South having managed to zig and zag themselves into the wrong contract on the last ten or so deals, now find this treat awaiting them. True to form, the bidding goes:

1♠	Pass	2♠	3♥
?			

South, having gone down in four spades moments before, thinks to himself,

"If partner has the wrong hand for the raise, I won't be able to make four spades; but if I bid three spades, then perhaps North will bid four, with a maximum hand." So it goes,

1♠	Pass	2♠	3♥
3♠	All Pass		

RESULT: Three spades making six. South suggested North should have bid four spades. North suggested South should have bid four spades. South pointed out that on the previous hand he had bid four spades and it had gone down when the dummy had a minimum. North of course replied that South might have had a much worse hand. After all, hadn't he held some pretty bad hands which were bid in the same way in the past?

This argument could go on and on, ending nowhere; but it can take a long time to get there. And the answer to this problem, and to many problems is so simple! Know your system and stick to it. I've said it before and I will surely repeat it again . .

The part about this that I find most confusing is that I know the players involved realize what their bids mean when they make them. I've asked my students what the bids should mean, and when asked, they knew. So it's clear that players make these bids in spite of knowing better. The errors are not made from ignorance.

Earlier I said that I could not understand why certain mistakes were made, but perhaps I do. If I'm right, perhaps you will recognize yourself; and if I'm wrong, well perhaps you'll recognize someone else.

This is the reason. People who play bridge do so in order to be doing something. Passing is not a form of doing, it is a form of laziness. Perhaps this urge to do something is so strong as to blind the player to the true meaning of a bid. Or perhaps the urge drives one to make the bid hoping that partner will pass it, or perhaps even hoping partner will forget it is supposed to be a strong bid.

Now it becomes a game of wishful thinking or dreams. When you have a good hand you wish partner to guess to bid a game when he has a good hand. And when you have made an overbid, you mentally will partner to pass regardless of what he has.

Quite confusing and quite impossible. So much easier to do it right and not have to hope partner can guess which way you are vacillating at any given time.

So . . . learn your system. Then stick to it. If your hand calls for a pass, then pass. Don't bid and then hope your partner passes. That's not bridge. That's just ridiculous.

When you learn to pass, your partner will learn to respect the times when you bid. You will then have achieved a partnership harmony, or rapport. When you have this, you will avoid unnecessary overbids and you will avoid silly underbids. You will be a pair, a partnership, and you will win. Even two experts who don't trust each other can't beat two average players who do.

The Modern Approach

I said that in some areas there are modern treatments . .
This is one of them.

The modern treatment recognizes that people like to bid. Now they have an excuse. Here it is in a nutshell.

When the bidding goes:

| 1♠ | 2♠ | or | 1♥ | 2♥ |
| 3♠ | | | 3♥ | |

| or | 1♥ | Pass | 2♥ | 2♠ | or | 1♠ | 2♥ | 2♠ | 3♥ |
| | 3♥ | | | | | 3♠ | | | |

it is not considered invitational. It is supposed to describe a hand that wants to play in exactly three hearts or three spades. Partner is expected to pass no matter what he has for his raise.

How then can the opening bidder ask of partner what kind of raise he has? Well, modern science has the answer. You must make a game try by bidding another suit. Here are a few sample auctions:

| 1♠ | 2♠ | 1♥ | 2♥ |
| 3♥ | | 3♣ | |

| 1♥ | Pass | 2♥ | 3♣ | 1♠ | 2♦ | 2♠ | 3♦ |
| 3♦ | | | | 3♥ | | | |

Sometimes you must make a game-try bid in a suit you don't really have. Look at the last auction. If you play that three spades would be a signoff bid, then three hearts is your only bid to invite partner to make an intelligent decision.

Now, when you make game tries, you try to bid a suit where you need some helping cards from partner's hand. But in the last example, you must bid three hearts as your game try regardless of whether or not you need help in hearts.

Perhaps you've noticed that in some instances this system falls apart, or at least appears to. For example, if this is the auction,

| 1♠ | 2♥ | 2♠ | 3♥ |
| ? | | | |

how can the modern scientist ask his partner if he has a maximum raise? Certainly, if a three spade bid shows a lack of game interest, you can't bid that when you *do* have an interest in game. So what do you do?

Fortunately, science is versatile and it has the answer, or at least it has a possible answer. It is this: "When there is no suit possible to bid for a game try, then use 'double' as a substitute."

1♠	2♥	2♠	3♥
DBL			

or

1♥	P	2♥	3♦
DBL			

or

1♥	2♦	2♥	3♦
DBL			

The doubles here are no longer for penalty. They are artificial bids which ask partner if he has a maximum for his raise.

What do you do when you want to double the opponents for penalty? Well, believe it or not, you can't.

In this auction,

1♠	2♥	2♠	3♥
?			

a three spade bid says you don't have a good hand, and a double is not for penalty! Is it all worth it?

My advice is to ignore the modern treatment completely. At its very best, it may possibly be better than the orthodox treatment, but the number of potential disasters here just do not warrant its use. All you need is one little forgetful moment, and the partnership will be unsure of itself forever. If you, for instance, can make five spades, imagine your pleasure as the opponents score an overtrick at three hearts doubled. I repeat — is it worth it?

Back to standard bridge and unconscious overbidding, continued.

Responding to Takeout Doubles

The second area of overbidding is almost as common as the first area just discussed, but it can be much more volatile. It is responding to takeout doubles and subsequent bids by the takeout doubler.

This area is particularly interesting because it demonstrates the law of compensation so well and so often.

The law of compensation? It is not really a law so much as it is a way of life at the bridge table. In the area of takeout doubles it works this way. The player responding to his partner's double seems on the average to underbid by about four points, but this is compensated for by the doubler who seems to overbid by about the same four points.

In practice it looks like this. South, in the following hand, opens one club. East and West then bid the hands as indicated. Do you agree with the auction? If you don't agree, how should the bidding have gone?

WEST	EAST
♠ KQJ7	♠ A6542
♥ A432	♥ K97
♦ 1087	♦ Q7
♣ K7	♣ 863

North	East	South	West	
—	—	1♣	DBL	Declarer made an overtrick. Does
Pass	1♠	Pass	2♠	this mean the bidding was proper? If not, who did the wrong thing?
All pass				For starters, the final contract was impeccable. But the bidding

was not. East and West made four bids during the auction. They were double, one spade, two spades, and the final pass. One of these bids was quite proper. The other three were quite improper, in fact downright awful. But the fact is that the three wrong bids would be made by a large number of people.

In order to understand what went wrong with the bidding I'm going to spend a lot of time on this hand. It's important enough to know what went wrong, but it is far and away more important to know why.

We can start with the first bid. Is West's double of one club legitimate or not? Should he have bid something else or not? If so, what?

After a one club bid, the only reasonable choice on this hand is double. The hand is clearly worth a bid and the distribution is right. Nothing else should be considered. So the auction is off to a fine start. However . . .

Here is East's hand again:

♠ A6542
♥ K97
♦ Q7
♣ 863

Now he must find a response to the double. The actual bid chosen was one spade, but as you may have gathered, it was not correct. So what's wrong with one spade?

To get to the answer one must first answer a few other questions. 1) How much is the hand worth? It is worth nine in high card points and one for the doubleton diamond. As a rule of thumb, you may also add another point when you have five cards in one of the suits that partner is asking about. So your hand is worth about eleven points. 2) What would you bid if your hand were, instead:

♠ K10764	or	♠ QJ863	or	♠ J1076
♥ 762		♥ 42		♥ 842
♦ 763		♦ 73		♦ 93
♣ K3		♣ J1063		♣ 10873

or	♠ 10653	or	♠ 8642
	♥ 42		♥ 873
	♦ 76		♦ 976
	♣ 75432		♣ 542

Would you bid one spade on all of them? Surely it can't be right to bid one spade on

♠ A6542	and also on	♠ 8642
♥ K97		♥ 873
♦ Q7		♦ 976
♣ 863		♣ 542

There must be some way of telling partner which hand you have. And there is.

Here are the various bids you can make in response to a takeout double. Beginning at the bottom of the list is the weakest possible response. It is a non-jump bid in any of the three remaining suits.

North	East	South	West
1♣	DBL	Pass	1♥
1♠	DBL	Pass	2♥
1♠	DBL	Pass	2♣
1♦	DBL	Pass	2♣
1♦	DBL	Pass	1♥

None of these responses were jump bids. They are all signoff bids. While it is true that this "signoff" may be made on hands worth as much as seven or eight points, it is possible, and perhaps likely, that responder has zero.

In response to partner's takeout double of one heart, these next hands would all be minimum responses. Notice the range for the simple signoff response.

♠ 8764
♥ 10862
♦ J3
♣ 1076

One spade. A terrible hand, admittedly.

♠ K7642
♥ 973
♦ J104
♣ 83

One spade. Still a minimum, but look how much better it is than the previous hand.

♠ AQ1076
♥ J2
♦ 1086
♣ 1084

One spade again. Just about as much as you can have to respond with one spade only.

♠ 82
♥ 76543
♦ 54
♣ J1076

Two clubs. The bid is not a jump, so it still falls in the minimum range. Even though the response is at the two level, no points are promised when responding to takeout double.

♠ 543
♥ 1076
♦ 5432
♣ KQ106

Two clubs again. A better hand this time.

♠ 543
♥ J7
♦ J54
♣ AQ862

Even better, but still only a two club response.

An important point to note here is that a *bid* is the weakest course of action you can take. Should you pass, you are actually taking a positive action, saying that you are *expecting* to defeat the opponents. You should not pass from fear. The kind of hand you should pass after partner has doubled one heart looks something like this:

♠ 42
♥ KQJ108
♦ J1076
♣ 108

or
		or	
♠ K7			♠ A3
♥ J109876			♥ AJ10876
♦ Q86			♦ 7642
♣ 102			♣ 3

A pass by you shows good trumps. Remember that. Something like five to the KQJ108 is a good whereas K76542 is terrible. Declarer is going to have the rest of the suit sitting over you. If you have bad trumps you won't be able to keep him from making quite a few trump tricks.

So what do you do when you have a bunch of trumps and nothing else? Why not pass and hope for the best? This question is easy to answer. If you let the opponents play in one heart doubled just because you have a bad hand, it will probably cost you the following:

1) Sixty points below the line, which may prove to be a thorn in your side during ensuing hands,

2) Fifty points for the "insult."

3) From 100 to 800 points in overtricks.

4) A partner.

So in this case, the less you have the more reason to find a bid, whatever it may be. After all, you haven't been doubled — yet.

Normally when you have one of these terrible hands you will have no problem finding a bid, once you have resolved that you *will* find one. But once in a while you may come across a hand calculated to weaken your resolve. It will probably look like one of these delightful hands below. Your bid. Remember the resolution.

♠ 8742	One spade. This one is easy. You
♥ 976542	have four of the other major, which
♦ 83	is one of the things partner wants.
♣ 10	

♠ 4	Two diamonds. This isn't guaranteed
♥ 108765	to work, but one heart doubled will
♦ 5432	not be good for you.
♣ J76	

♠ 1086	This is the worst. A completely
♥ J8742	unnecessary aggravation in one's
♦ 64	bridge career. No one needs this.
♣ 974	But life goes on and you are going
	to have to decide what to do. Keeping

in mind the resolve that it's right to bid something, you decide to bid. But what? You can't bid one notrump. That guarantees something (see the next section), so you will have to choose between one spade and two clubs. If it bothers you to bid a three card suit, pretend that partner over there has bid both of them and you are merely giving a preference bid. We all agree that neither one spade nor two clubs is anyone's idea of perfection, but what is? So which will it be?

You can bid one spade on the theory that it keeps the bidding lower. Or you can bid two clubs on the theory that partner will be less enthusiastic over this than over one spade. I myself prefer one spade. You may prefer two clubs. The only thing that is 100% sure is that you *cannot* pass. That would be an honest-to-goodness disaster.

THE ONE NOTRUMP RESPONSE

The next bid on the ladder of responses to a takeout double is one notrump. Unfortunately this is a very vague bid and nowhere have I found a satisfactory description. In fact, I doubt that there is one.

Generally speaking though, you will find that these principles hold true. When your partner doubles, he is usually interested in hearing you respond in a major suit if you have one.

RULE: If you bid one notrump, you are denying a four card major. If you do conceal a major suit, it will frequently lead to a missed game or perhaps the wrong game. This can be expensive. Partscore bidding may also suffer, and while partscore disasters may not be as spectacular as game disasters, they too can add up.

If partner doubled one club, you would respond as indicated:

♠ Q1076	One spade. Not one notrump. Bid
♥ 84	a major suit in preference to one
♦ 973	notrump whenever possible.
♣ K962	

♠ 42	One heart. Don't worry about the
♥ 9876	poor quality of your suit. All you
♦ J76	promised was four of them. (Remem-
♣ AJ52	ber that with some really hopeless
	hands you may have to make this bid

with only three of them.)

The next consideration is how many points the bid shows. Ask yourself this. If you had eighteen points with balanced distribution, for instance:

♠ KQ107	and you doubled one club, would
♥ AQ54	you think of bidding a game if
♦ KQ7	partner responded one notrump?
♣ Q9	

What do you think he has? Does he have eight or nine points, in which case you may have a game? Does he have nothing at all? Does he have a club stopper? Well? Do you have any idea? It is clear that you should have some understanding as to what values the bid shows.

I suggest that you play somewhat along these lines:
1) The bid should show a stopper in the opponents' suit.

If your partner can't count on you to produce a stopper, then you won't be able to get to game on quite a few occasions when it is right. In a pinch you might do it on 10764 or J106, but you should strain to avoid it.

2) The bid of one notrump should promise about six to ten high card points. There are two reasons for this. The first is that your partner will be able to judge what your side can make when he knows your point range. His decision-making will be much easier if he knows you have 6 to 10 as opposed to zero to ten.

The second reason is common sense. One notrump is a very easy contract for the opponents to double. You will need those six or more points to avoid getting killed by the opponents. After all, if your partner makes a double with 13 or 14 points, you won't want to end up in one notrump doubled if you have only one, two, or even three points yourself.

This is why you should not be bidding one notrump in response to partner's double of one heart on: ♠ 1086, ♥ J8742, ♦ 64, ♣ 974. Remember this hand? It is from the earlier section on minimum responses to a takeout double. At the time I stated as a fact that you shouldn't bid one notrump because the hand wasn't good enough. Now you know why it is necessary to have more than this for that bid.

If you follow the suggestions for bidding one notrump, you will find that many of the hands on which there used to be problems will now be bid easily and reasonably accurately. Indeed you will still have some problems, but they will usually occur only on the genuinely bad hands. They will still be problems. Whatever you do may work, or it may not work. You may go down 1100, but you might have gone down 1100 no matter what you did. What *will* happen is that when you or partner bids one notrump, you will have an understanding as to its meaning. As a result, many of your auctions will lose their haphazard and indeterminate nature. Also, you will receive fewer lessons from the kibitzer.

Quite some time ago, this hand and auction were presented for criticism:

West	East				
♠ KQJ7	♠ A6542	West	North	East	South
♥ A432	♥ K97	—	—	—	1♣
♦ 1083	♦ Q7	DBL	Pass	1♠	Pass
♣ K7	♣ 863	2♠	All Pass		

Declarer actually made nine tricks, which was no problem. However, the bidding left something to be desired.

So far, it is apparent that the double was quite correct; but the one spade bid was wrong. That bid is a signoff bid showing a maximum of seven or eight points.

What, then, is the correct bid? Did you say two spades? Yes? Well, two spades is the correct bid 100%. But the reasons for the bid being correct are as important as the bid itself. Wnat does two spades show? Is it forcing to game? Does it promise a five card suit? Is it a slam try?

As it turns out, the answer to all of these questions is *NO*. The bid shows a hand worth from nine to eleven points in support of the suit bid. It shows a minimum of a good four card suit. If the suit is five cards, the quality doesn't matter. It is *not* a forcing bid. The doubler is welcome to pass if he holds a minimum double.

Notice that this bid is a jump. It was possible to bid one spade, but the bid chosen was two spades. Notice also that it was a single jump. A jump to three spades would be a double jump. This would have yet another meaning. Here are some typical examples:

1♣	DBL	Pass	2♠
1♥	DBL	Pass	2♠
1♥	DBL	Pass	3♣
1♠	DBL	Pass	3♦
1♠	DBL	Pass	3♥

They are all single jumps describing about nine to eleven points. They are all invitational only. They are *not* forcing.

Here are some hands. Partner has doubled one heart.

♠ AKJ7
♥ 982
♦ Q1094
♣ 107

Two spades. A good four card suit and the hand is worth eleven points.

♠ KJ107
♥ A962
♦ 43
♣ Q105

Two spades. Similar to the above.

♠ Q9764
♥ 10652
♦ A5
♣ Q9

Two spades. This hand is worth eleven points. Remember to add one point for the five card suit.

♠ 76542
♥ J73
♦ AQ5
♣ K3

Two spades. *Any* five card major is worth a jump if the hand is good enough.

♠ Q1082
♥ 8763
♦ AK7
♣ Q2

Two spades. The suit is not quite up to standards but the hand is maximum in terms of points.

♠ 42 ♥ 932 ♦ KQ7 ♣ AJ864	Three clubs. When jumping in a minor suit, you should usually have a five card suit.

If you have a minor suit, it may be reasonable to bid an appropriate number of notrump. Although you would not conceal a four card major, it is quite all right to suppress four or even five card minor suits in order to bid notrump.

♠ 73 ♥ K107 ♦ J96 ♣ A8642	One notrump. Even though the hand is worth ten points in support of clubs, one notrump is a better call.

The hands which will give you the most problems are the ones which include a bad major suit but have quite a few points.
Partner doubles one heart. You have:

♠ 8762 ♥ A42 ♦ K42 ♣ KJ3	I think I would bid two spades. It's not wonderful, but if partner has much extra, we should have a good chance for game. I don't blame you for objecting to a jump on this

suit, but hopefully partner has some spade support. He did suggest it. If this seems in contradiction to the rule that you need at least a good four card suit to jump, it is. But it's one of those areas where nothing works all the time. Certainly, you'd like to have a better suit.

♠ 9642 ♥ 432 ♦ AK7 ♣ K108	One spade. This is a maximum for a one spade response, but when the suit is as bad as this, you should deduct one point. The distribution is also vile.

Here is a good rule of thumb. If you think you may have a game opposite a reasonable fifteen points, then you should jump. As will be seen later, partner will raise a simple non-jump response only if he has at least fifteen points. Here is another useful rule. **RULE: When an opponent has opened the bidding, your side can reasonably look for game with only twenty-four points instead of the usual twenty-five or twenty-six.** This is because you can take advantage of the fact that you know where most of the high cards are. Frequently you can gain a trick in the play as a result of being able to locate the missing points.

This rule is mentioned now because of the number of potential games your side may bid after the auction begins in the way we've been discussing.

When someone doubles and the responder jumps, then a game is likely. A player who is aware of the above rule may be able to bid and make quite a few extra games which might not ordinarily be bid. Even in those cases when the responder makes a signoff response, if the doubler can make a game invitation the partnership should again aim for the aggressive game contracts. Whenever you have reason to know where the outstanding high cards are located it pays to bid the close games.

With all this in mind, it is time to get back to the doubler. It is much easier to discuss his problems. Usually the doubler will pass whatever his partner has bid, unless he thinks there may be a game. In this case the doubler can raise responder or perhaps even jump to game if his hand warrants. But whatever is done, it is done IN LIGHT OF WHAT THE RESPONDER HAS BID.

If the responder has made a minimum bid, a simple raise by the doubler asks if responder has the maximum for his bid. Do you remember what the maximum was?

South	West	North	East
1♦	DBL	Pass	1♠

How much did one spade guarantee? It showed from zero to eight points. Therefore, the doubler needs at least sixteen points to hope for a game. If the bidding proceeds

South	West	North	East
1♦	DBL	Pass	1♠
Pass	2♠		

then West is showing from 16 to 18 points. Responder is invited to consider bidding again if he has the maximum possible for what he has shown. If he has seven or eight, it should produce a game.

For example:

West	East
♠ KJ76	♠ A10432
♥ A1086	♥ Q73
♦ AQ62	♦ 85
♣ 10	♣ J43

South	West	North	East	
1♣	DBL	Pass	1♠	West has a nice 17 points in
Pass	2♠	Pass	4♠	support of spades. Two spades

shows this hand and asks East if he has a maximum for his one spade bid. East has a maximum and a five card suit as well. Four spades, though on only twenty-one high card points, will likely make an overtrick.

West did not raise to two spades just to show he had some spade support. The original double showed that. The raise to two spades confirms that support and it shows a better-than-average double.

Sometimes the doubler has more than eighteen. Perhaps he has nineteen, twenty, or even twenty-one. When this is the case, I usually see the doubler jump right to game. This is nice when partner has five or so points. It is not so nice when partner doesn't have them. In the latter case, declarer goes down a few tricks and the dummy says, "I hoped you had something." Declarer then shakes his head sadly and agrees that it would have been nice but this time he was broke. Too bad.

This is not necessary. If you have twenty points, it is clear that you can't guarantee a game. You would want to find out if partner were broke or if in fact he did have a morsel or two. This fact can be found out by asking partner, "Do you have anything at all?" Bridgewise, this is done by jump-raising the response:

South	West	North	East
1♣	DBL	Pass	1♥
Pass	3♥		

The jump raise raise shows the nineteen to twenty-one point hand. It asks partner if he has five or more points and, if so, to bid a game. This raise is an invitational bid, and is *not* forcing. Responder may pass any time he has a genuinely bad hand.

Using the above auction, let me show you some examples:

West	East	
♠ AQ107	♠ J3	Here East has six points and
♥ AKJ4	♥ Q1052	should be happy to bid four
♦ K876	♦ QJ103	hearts.
♣ 4	♣ 1064	

East	
♠ 9	Believe it or not, this hand
♥ 106532	should bid four hearts. It is
♦ Q108	worth at least six points (one
♣ 8765	for the extra heart).

East	
♠ 765	
♥ 9842	
♦ 1093	
♣ K97	

This is a clear cut pass. Even though you have more high cards than the previous hand, this is not even worth a second look. Pass.

42

Bidding these hands this way requires that you and partner trust each other. When the doubler jumps to three hearts, as in the previous hand, he is trusting his partner to go to game with almost any excuse at all. On the other hand, East has to trust his partner to have what he promises.

I said East should bid four hearts with, ♠ 9, ♥ 106532, ♦ Q108, ♣ 8765. If East does bid four hearts, as he should, then it behooves West to have his twenty points as advertised. It is definitely a partnership game. This particular partnership is going to do well because on those hands where three hearts is the limit, they will be in three making, rather than rashly bidding to game.

Once in a while you have such a big hand that you want to be in game no matter what partner has. How do you get to game if this is the case? The answer here is . . . . . bid it. The only mistake you can make is to jump to the three level. As I said before, this bid is invitational only. If you know you have a game no matter what, then bid it.

These hands are typical for an immediate jump to game.

South	West	North	East
1♥	DBL	Pass	1♠
Pass	4♠	All pass	

West might have:

West		West		West
♠ KQJ7	or	♠ J10876	or	♠ QJ108
♥ 8		♥ A		♥ AK
♦ AKJ97		♦ AK10		♦ A106
♣ AQ2		♣ AQ42		♣ AKJ3

If partner has nothing but four or five small spades, then there will be a reasonable shot at game. Don't make the error of jumping to three spades only. That jump is not forcing.

You may have noticed I did not discuss two additional possible responses to the takeout double. They are 1) A jump to two or three notrump; and 2) A cue bid of the doubled suit.

The reason these bids were not covered in depth is that they are seldom misused. The purpose of this book is to clear up common errors. Such in those situations is not the case.

A definition of those bids is given here, but only to put the rest of this discussion in perspective. A jump to two notrump shows eleven or twelve high card points. It denies a four card major suit and it guarantees a stopper in the doubled suit. This bid is not forcing! It is an invitational bid, and partner may pass if he has a minimum double.

The cue bid is the only bid you have which says, "Partner, we must get to game." Once a cue bid has been made in response to a takeout double, the partnership must continue bidding until game has been reached.

In the following deals there are a few hands covering the above areas, but that will be all. As I said, those bids don't require a lot of space in this book. There are other more important problems to consider.

This section, as you may remember, started by discussing some of the more common overbidding (and underbidding) practices. If it seems that I digress a bit into takeout doubles and responses to them, it was for a good reason. In no other area of bidding are so many overbids and underbids made.

A long time was spent in evaluating the bidding of the first hand in the list below. It was necessary. Now try doing the same thing for the rest of the hands. Do you approve of the bidding? If not, what else would have been better? Pay particular attention to the "law of compensation." (This is, to save you from back reference, the tendency of one player to overbid by some amount in the hope that partner is underbidding by a like amount.)

West	East				
♠ KQJ7	♠ A6542	West	North	East	South
♥ A432	♥ K97	—	—	—	1♣
♦ 1083	♦ Q7	DBL	Pass	1♠	Pass
♣ K7	♣ 863	2♠	All pass		

This made three spades. Everything OK?

As has been seen, everything was not okay. Responder has eleven points. It is enough to jump to two spades. One spade was a gross underbid. The raise to two spades should show at least 16 points. This hand is worth at most fourteen. Two spades is an overbid. The final pass is again an amazing underbid. The hand should clearly be worth a jump to four spades. If partner had his promised 16 points, game should be easy to make; but partner didn't and game was impossible. The law of compensation was never better demonstrated.

West	East				
♠ AJ86	♠ 9742	West	North	East	South
♥ KJ97	♥ 103	—	—	—	1♣
♦ AQ106	♦ 872	DBL	Pass	1♠	Pass
♣ 2	♣ K985	3♠	All pass		

Down one in three spades. Unlucky? No. Someone bid too much. The double is fine; and the one spade response is correct. Don't even think of one notrump. However, the three spade bid is an overbid. A raise to two spades would describe the West hand. This hand is worth eighteen points which is within the 16 to 18 point range of a simple raise. This is another case of the law of compensations not working. East had a truly bad hand and West's overbid was properly punished.

West	East				
♠ KQ76	♠ 10852	West	North	East	South
♥ QJ97	♥ 63	—	—	—	1♣
♦ A874	♦ Q2	DBL	Pass	1NT	All pass
♣ 7	♣ A6543				

This was down one. Two spades is cold. Who goofed?

This one is easy. East has a clear cut bid of one spade. Certainly the spade suit is not very good; but then, neither is going down in one notrump very good. West was completely blameless. This double was a normal aggressive bid which should have led to a spade partscore. Remember to bid those major suits!

West	East				
♠ KJ8	♠ 73	West	North	East	South
♥ AQ107	♥ 9642	—	—	—	1♣
♦ KQJ8	♦ 93	DBL	All pass		
♣ 42	♣ J10876				

An overtrick was made. East could have made one or two hearts. What went wrong? East again. When you pass a takeout double, you do so because you *expect* to defeat the opponents. You don't pass just because you don't like your hand. The East hand should bid one heart. This doesn't promise a single point and West won't expect East to produce any. Of course, West may *hope* that East has something, but that is all West is entitled to do — hope.

West	East				
♠ J764	♠ 8532	West	North	East	South
♥ AQ76	♥ K3	—	—	—	1♣
♦ KQ8	♦ 764	DBL	Pass	1♠	2♣
♣ Q4	♣ 9862	2♠	DBL	All pass	

Two clubs would have made, but two spades doubled went down three. This was no bargain. Your opinion?

This is yet another example of the law of compensation . . . at its worst. At the end of this hand West complained of his ill luck. How could East have such bad cards, etc. What happened, of course, is that West made a gross overbid and East failed to come up with the extra "hoped for" cards.

What West forgot was that East is still allowed to do something. If West passes two clubs, as he should with his minimum double, then East could: 1) Pass when he had a bad hand, 2) Bid something if he had a maximum for his one spade bid, or 3) Double if he saw fit. West, by bidding, makes it impossible for East to do anything reasonable.

West	East				
♠ AQ72	♠ J10642	West	North	East	South
♥ AQJ8	♥ 107	—	—	—	1♣
♦ Q1073	♦ AJ8	DBL	Pass	1♠	2♣
♣ 2	♣ 1083	2♠	Pass	3♠	Pass
		4♠	All pass		

This made exactly, but was the bidding correct? For a change the bidding was completely right by everyone. East's response of one spade is all the hand is worth. West's raise to two spades shows 16 to 18 points with four card trump support. East can anticipate making a game if West has the maximum of his 16 to 18 point range. His three spade bid says "if you have a maximum, in terms of what you've already shown, then bid four spades. Otherwise pass." West does have a maximum and can go on to game. This hand was well bid on both sides of the table.

West	East				
♠ K32	♠ Q108	West	North	East	South
♥ AJ107	♥ Q2	—	—	—	1♣
♦ 986	♦ A1073	DBL	Pass	1♦	Pass
♣ KQ2	♣ 10763	1NT	All pass		

This made exactly. Do you concur with the bidding? I hope not.

The double by West is marginal — there is too much stuff in clubs and not enough elsewhere to warrant a takeout double (to say nothing of the distribution). East might have bid notrump, but the diamond response is acceptable. One notrump by West? NO NO NO. When you double, and then after partner responds, you bid one notrump, you guarantee a full one notrump bid. It's just as though you overcalled one notrump. The only difference is that first you chose to look for a suit fit.

When you overcall one notrump after the opponents open, you need a good hand. After all, your partner may have a bad hand and you will be in serious trouble. So whether you make a notrump overcall or rebid a notrump after doubling, you (i.e., West) must have at least 16 points. Remember this.

Getting back to the hand, East was very guilty of underbidding. If West really does have 16 to 18 points to justify the one notrump bid, then East should consider a game contract.

East				
♠ Q108	West	North	East	South
♥ Q2	—	—	—	1♣
♦ A1073	DBL	Pass	1♦	Pass
♣ 10763	1NT	Pass	?	

East should bid at least two notrump. This invites game if West has a maximum. If, however, you wanted to be aggressive, you might even jump to three notrump with the East hand. Remember the rule. When the opponents have opened, you may bid games more aggressively because you usually can take advantage of knowing where the points are located.

West	East				
♠ J97	♠ 43	West	North	East	South
♥ 10864	♥ A9	—	—	—	1♣
♦ AKQ10	♦ J864	DBL	Pass	2NT	All pass
♣ K4	♣ AQ62				

Two notrump made on the nose. Comments? None. The double was reasonable and the response quite correct. The jump to two notrump shows eleven or twelve points. West had a minimum double and decided to reject East's invitation.

West	East				
♠ AJ72	♠ 43	West	North	East	South
♥ K1093	♥ 873	—	—	—	1♣
♦ J2	♦ 109874	DBL	Pass	1♦	2♣
♣ AQ3	♣ J32	2NT	DBL	All pass	

This was too bloody for words. Down 1400. Declarer took exactly three tricks.

What happened here was just completely unnecessary. Earlier I said that a one notrump overcall shows 16 to 18 points. Here West, who did not have enough to bid *one* notrump, later took it upon himself to contract for *two* notrump. West isn't overbidding by just one or two points, he is overbidding by six or seven. This is the law of compensation again producing a terrible result. West overbid by seven points and this time East could only produce *one*.

West	East				
♠ A876	♠ K1095	West	North	East	South
♥ AKJ7	♥ Q2	—	—	—	1♣
♦ Q103	♦ AKJ7	DBL	Pass	2♣	Pass
♣ 92	♣ 1063	2♥	Pass	2♠	Pass
		3♠	Pass	4♠	All pass

Four spades bid and made. This is an example of the cue bid in action. East has a hand good enough to play in game, but where? It might be right to play in four spades, three notrump, or even five diamonds. The cue bid says, "We have enough to play in game somewhere. Let's start bidding suits, keeping three notrump open."

West obliges by showing his hearts. East replies by showing his spades. As East has already forced to game, it is no longer necessary to jump. West has an easy raise to three spades and East continues to game.

The principle to recognize here is that the cue bid is unconditionally forcing to game. This allows both players to describe their hands accurately. West, for instance, may be able to rebid a five card heart suit, or East may show five spades by rebidding them.

West	East				
♠ AQ72	♠ J5	West	North	East	South
♥ Q108	♥ A93	—	—	—	1♣
♦ A1076	♦ KQ952	DBL	Pass	3NT	Pass
♣ 93	♣ QJ5	Pass	Pass		

Declarer took ten tricks. Reasonably bid? Well bid all around.

West has a minimum, but reasonable, double, East has enough for game and he has a good idea where he wants to play. In fact, East *knows* where he wants to play the hand. East wants to play in three notrump, and the way to get there is to bid it. Which he did.

The mistakes to avoid with the East hand are: 1) Don't jump to two diamonds and 2) Don't jump to two notrump. Neither of these bids is forcing. If East chooses to make either of these two bids he will likely find himself passed out in that contract. For the actual hand, West has a minimum and clearly can't find a bid after any *non-forcing* response.

RULE: If you know you can make a game, either bid it or make a cue bid which forces the partnership to get there eventually.

West	East				
♠ KJ87	♠ Q10642	West	North	East	South
♥ A1074	♥ K32	—	—	—	1♣
♦ K1082	♦ 974	DBL	Pass	1♠	3♣
♣ 2	♣ J2	3♠	4♣	4♠	DBL
		All pass.			

Down two. Who bid too much? This is again West's fault, which is no surprise. As is usually the case, it is the takeout doubler who eventually bids too much. It is seldom the responder.

Why is this? There is a good psychological explanation for this situation and therefore for this mistake. When someone makes a takeout double, they are not thinking of it as a *bid* so much as they are thinking of it as a request for partner to bid. When partner does bid, as requested, the doubler mentally says to himself "partner has *bid*" whereas partner has not really bid at all. He has answered a question that he had to answer.

Rightly or wrongly, the doubler then assigns some values to partner's "bid" because most bids to tend to show something. Not only that, but usually the "bid" is in a suit for which the doubler has good support. No surprise, of course, because the double asked for that suit and partner was merely obliging.

The doubler forgets all this though, and thinks it is nice that he has a good hand and support for partner. So he raises, forgetting that he has already shown his hand with the original double. Actually, the doubler is not raising his partner, he is raising himself! This is what happened in the hand under discussion. West doubled one club holding:

West
♠ KJ87
♥ A1074
♦ K1082
♣ 2

East responded one spade. The opening bidder bid three clubs and West had a common problem. Should he or shouldn't he? Three spades or pass?

If West bids three spades he is showing a much better than average double. Something like eighteen points is about right. Is this hand good enough to bid three spades? I think not.

From the East position, would you bid four spades on

East
♠ Q10642
♥ K72
♦ 974
♣ J2

when the bidding has gone:

West	North	East	South
—	—	—	1♣
Dbl	Pass	1♠	3♣
3♠	Pass	?	

Actually, you should. If your partner has his bid your hand is well worth going on to game.

What is your hand worth? It is worth five in high card points, one for the fifth spade, and perhaps one for the doubleton club. Don't count that club jack for anything; but even discarding that card, your hand is easily worth seven points. Opposite the eighteen (or more) West ought to have, East would be a bit cowardly to pass. In fact, a pass would be more craven than a bid of four spades would be courageous.

So far in this discussion the problem you've been dealing with has been concerned with this auction only:

1X -DBL -Pass? (X referring to any of the four suits.)

What happens when the auction has changed so that the opponents have bid two suits? Auctions like these:

1♣	Pass	1♥	DBL
1♦	Pass	1♠	DBL
1♠	Pass	2♣	DBL
1♦	Pass	2♣	DBL

For the most part the responder's considerations are the same as in the previous situations when the opponents bid only one suit. The weakest bid responder can make is a non-jump bid in one of the two suits the double calls for. This remains the same. A jump still shows about ten points and is still non-forcing. It asks partner to pass with a minimum or to bid on with a maximum.

The one bid which is changed is the one notrump bid. When partner doubles after two suits have been bid, a one notrump bid can be made on as little as four points instead of the six or seven you normally want. Do you see why?

The reason is quite logical. When partner doubles the opening bid, you have three suits to choose from. It is very likely that you will have one to bid. But when partner doubles after two suits have been bid, there remain only two suits for you. The chances are that you will be able to bid one of them, but there will be times when you have five-four-two-two distribution. If partner has doubled, showing the suits in which you hold two each only (and don't tell me it doesn't happen), then the least disastrous course available to you is to bid one notrump. Bidding a two card suit is just a little bit rich. This is why one notrump may be used as an escape bid when partner has doubled after two suits have been bid.

What is your bid on the following hands? What is your reasoning? Some of these are real stinkers. If you can handle them, you can handle anything. You are East.

East
♠ KJ97
♥ A6432
♦ J7
♣ 93

West	North	East	South
—	1♣	Pass	1♥
DBL	Pass	?	

Two spades, just like the earlier auctions. You have eleven points and a good four card major. Don't make the mistake of passing one heart or of bidding only one spade.

East
♠ 106542
♥ A652
♦ K8
♣ 103

West	North	East	South
—	1♣	Pass	1♥
DBL	Pass	?	

Two spades again. Remember to add one point for the fifth card in a suit partner has asked you to bid. This hand is worth ten points.

	East	West	North	East	South
♠	64	West	North	East	South
♥	8652	—	1♣	Pass	1♦
♦	Q7	DBL	Pass	?	
♣	J9654				

One heart. This is a signoff bid. There is no promise of any high cards whatsoever.

	East	West	North	East	South
♠	765	West	North	East	South
♥	K10654	—	1♦	Pass	1♠
♦	Q2	DBL	Pass	?	
♣	832				

Two hearts. This is still a signoff bid. Even though the response is at the two level, there is still no guarantee of any points. You have made a non-jump response. In fact, this hand is quite nice, as you have a five card suit.

	East	West	North'	East	South
♠	1065	West	North'	East	South
♥	J642	—	1♣	Pass	1♥
♦	3	DBL	Pass	?	
♣	108652				

One spade. Unpleasant for sure, but you have to bid something. Passing is a sure route to disaster.

	East	West	North	East	South
♠	K1073	West	North	East	South
♥	42	—	1♣	Pass	1♠
♦	76	DBL	Pass	?	
♣	J6542				

One notrump. This is one of those hands that you hate to have, but it happens so you may as well try to be ready. It's possible that clubs might be the best suit for your side, but two clubs is a cue bid showing a good hand.

	East	West	North	East	South
♠	10864	West	North	East	South
♥	2	—	1♣	Pass	1♠
♦	87	DBL	Pass	?	
♣	J106542				

Scary, isn't it? Do you have any ideas about what to do? Well neither do I! I can only hope you never have to hold this hand. Why is this hand in here as a question? Partly, it's here as a mild jest. But seriously, I've included it in the hopes that you will more appreciate the rest of the hands you may have when the auction goes as indicated.

Free Bids

Continuing onward in the family of overbidding and underbidding, there is one last area of great importance. It belongs entirely in the family of underbidding.

This may seem a little strange, because few people like to admit to underbidding. Therefore, they must not know that they are. This area may seem familiar to you, since I have spent the last several pages covering something which may seem similar.

The area in question is the following: "Free bids by the player whose partner has made a takeout double." If that sounds impressive, it's because I can't think of a shorter title. The problem itself is very simple. When the bidding goes:

North	East	South	West	X = any bid
X	DBL	Y	?	Y = any bid

what do you need to make a free bid in response to the double? Some people will say seven points; some people will say ten points.

I am going to suggest that all this is incredibly conservative and that, with proper judgment, a free bid may be correct on four points in one case, while a free bid on seven points, in another case, may be wrong.

In fact this is one of the areas where points lose much of their luster. Decisions cannot be made on the basis of points alone. I will concede only that they may provide a vague guide. But the emphasis here is most surely on the word "vague."

Instead, you are going to have to apply a different form of evaluation known in the trade as judgment.

Your decision to bid or not to bid, will depend, in marginal cases, on the following.

(1) How good is the suit you intend to bid?

(2) How well placed are the few high cards you do have?

(3) At what level are you bidding? That is, can your bid be made at the one level, or must you bid higher?

Bear in mind that this section deals only with those marginal cases where it is not clear whether you should or should not bid. If you have quite a good hand, you will know that you want to bid, and the question instead is "what" to bid. Most players do not have problems in this area, so it won't be covered.

Why should there be much space devoted to this area? Why be concerned over little hands when the rewards are so small? You will not have to worry about a slam. Seldom will you ever have a game. In fact, the most likely involvement for you will be a partscore. Is it worth fighting for? Should there be a significant discussion here about partscore bidding, when, instead, there could be one on slam bidding? (On which topic, incidentally, I intend to spend little or no time.)

The answer to these questions is . . . yes, yes, yes, indeed.

Look at this simple arithmetic. Let us say that in one hundred hands, you have eight partscore decisions. If you sell out, and do not compete, your opponents may be allowed to score eight partscores on hands where *you* should have had the eight partscores.

This may mean that the opponents can combine then to make four games. This may be worth as much as 1500 points to the enemy. On the other hand, if you go out there and fight, you may get eight partscores yourself, and hence, the 1500 points. The swing is 3000 points. That is a lot. And it may be more. Every now and then you may set the opponents 800 when they foolishly try to stop you from converting a partscore into game.

Now let us assume you have, during these one hundred hands, three slam decisions. Let us say that on one hand, you do the right thing. On the second hand you miss a slam. This costs you 500 points. And on the third hand you go down in a slam you should never have bid. This costs you another 500 points. Perhaps it may cost a 1000 points. In any case, the three slams caused you to lose 1500 points.

Now I ask you this. In one hundred hands, which is more likely for you to have: eight partscore problems or three slam problems?

I suggest you are far more likely to have eight partscore problems than three slam problems. I would expect you to have something like twenty partscores and one or two slams. Which means that partscores cost an incredible amount relative to what slams cost. Perhaps ten times as much is lost in partscore bidding as in slam bidding. It is just harder to see a partscore loss than a spectacular slam loss.

I hope you're convinced. If so, you will pay more attention to this section than you might otherwise have done.

In these hands, the bidding goes as indicated. Your bid. As you answer the questions, try to get away from the concepts of "points." You'll see what I mean as you go from hand to hand.

Ready?

East

♠ 10653
♥ 875
♦ Q106
♣ J42

South	West	North	East
1♣	DBL	1♥	?

Pass of course. No possible reason to bid. Had North not bid one heart, you would have bid one spade. But you no longer have an obligation to bid, so if you do decide to do something, you must have a reason.

East
♠ KQ76   South West   North East
♥ 42   1♣   DBL   1♥   ?
♦ 10863
♣ 942

One spade. You have a good four card suit and you can compete at the one level.

East
♠ 10863   South West   North East
♥ 42   1♣   DBL   1♥   ?
♦ KQ76
♣ 942

Pass. Your spade suit is not so good this time. Note that in neither this nor the preceding hand should you consider bidding diamonds. When partner makes a takeout double you should strain to respond in a major suit.

East
♠ KJ864   South West   North East
♥ 763   1♣   DBL   1♥   ?
♦ 86
♣ 542

One spade. Quite a nice five card suit. Admittedly, you haven't much in the way of high cards, but they are well located. When you are responding to a takeout double, you must be aware that some high cards will be worth far more than others. Cards in the suits your partner has shown are worth much more than cards in the opponents' suits.

East
♠ 97654   South West   North East
♥ J32   1♣   DBL   1♥   ?
♦ 86
♣ K73

Here you have one king and one jack. You also have a five card spade suit. On the surface, the hand is worth the same as the preceding hand. Do you agree?
Look at these two side by side:

♠ KJ864   ♠ 97654   Are they really the same? No.
♥ 763   ♥ J32   Not even close. In the first
♦ 86   ♦ 86   case, the spade king and jack are
♣ 542   ♣ K73   working overtime. They are
guaranteed to be useful.

In the second case, your king and your jack are both in suits bid by the opponents. It is possible they may amount to something, but if they turned out to be worthless, it would be no surprise.

In the long run you will find that the first hand is worth at least twice as much as the second. And it could be worth more than that!

Let's go back to the original question. Did you bid with the second hand?

If you did bid one spade, I would say you had made an aggressive bid. I would also suggest you skip the rest of this chapter because I'm trying to encourage you to bid more in this situation. If you bid one spade, you obviously don't need any further encouragement.

As to the merits of bidding one spade, I wouldn't, but it is a close decision and it could easily work out. The fact that you could consider bidding one spade here should give you some idea of the extremes to which you may go in order to compete in a reasonable manner.

East
♠ 762
♥ KJ832
♦ 43
♣ 752

South	West	North	East
1♣	DBL	1♠	?

This is the same hand as in the previous example, but the suits have been changed slightly. In order to bid, you will have to do so at the two level. If you are tempted to bid two hearts here, your thinking is definitely going in the right direction; but bidding here is just a little bit overdoing things.

East
♠ 543
♥ AJ952
♦ J3
♣ 1043

South	West	North	East
1♣	DBL	1♠	?

Two hearts now. The hand has been strengthened by adding the diamond jack and by changing the heart king to the heart ace. This is really quite a solid two heart bid. That diamond jack is in one of the suits partner has shown and it is potentially quite valuable.

East
♠ 742
♥ A10642
♦ 73
♣ Q54

South	West	North	East
1♣	DBL	1♠	?

This is still worth a bid. I say "still" because the hand is not worth nearly as much as the preceding hand. Look at these two hands together:

♠ 543	♠ 742	Both of these hands have six
♥ AJ952	♥ A10642	points in high cards and they
♦ J3	♦ 73	have exactly the same distrib-
♣ 1043	♣ Q54	ution. But given the auction
		(Do you remember it without

peeking?) the hands are worlds apart in true worth. I would evaluate the first hand something like this: "I have six high card points and a useful doubleton. Therefore I start with seven points. My heart jack and my diamond jack both look to be useful. I will award the hand one more point to allow for this. I have also a five card suit. This is easily worth an additional point. Surely this hand is worth at least nine total points in terms of usefulness."

The second hand has also six high card points. My evaluation would run something like this: "I have six high card points plus one for the doubleton diamond and one for the five card suit. However, that queen of clubs may be completely useless. It looks like the defense will lead a spade and then switch to clubs through my queen. The only good thing about this queen of clubs is that I have it and it may prevent the opponents from leading clubs effectively at the start; but it is unlikely to be of much help later in the play. I certainly think it is worth no more than one point. Perhaps it is entirely worthless. This hand is then worth about six and one-half points."

Maybe it is being finicky to try to evaluate hands in terms of halves, but in close decisions these "halves" are what may cause you to go one way or another. In any case, the first hand is almost forty % better than the second hand.

There is a good exercise available to the enterprising reader. It will take a little while, but it should be worth the effort.

Make up twenty or so hands with which you would double an opening club bid. Now see how each of these two above hands "fits" opposite your takeout double hands. You should find the first hand is worth almost a trick more than the second.

The reason so much time is being spent here on evaluation is quite simple. When partner has doubled for takeout, it is very important to be able to judge what a hand is worth and how much action to take. It is a frequently recurring situation, so it behooves you to know how to value a hand under various circumstances.

Lastly, and most important, this is one of the few situations where you can actually correctly estimate the value of your hand early in the bidding. Here is the reason.

When partner doubles, he is defining his hand very accurately for you. Only a one notrump opening bid describes a hand as completely as does a takeout double. Compare some other typical bids and see how well, or poorly, they are defined.

One spade — opening bid.

This shows twelve to twenty-two points and guarantees four (or five or more) spades. Perhaps the distribution is 6-6-1-0, 5-3-3-2, 7-3-2-1, or 5-6-0-2. It may take two or three bids to completely describe the hand.

One spade — pass — one notrump.

The one notrump response shows six to nine points but may have some rather strange distributions.

One club — pass — one heart.

One heart shows from six to twenty points and four or more hearts. It can be bid on either of these hands:

♠ K72	or	♠ KJ87
♥ QJ72		♥ KQ10974
♦ 42		♦ 42
♣ J863		♣ A

What do these hands have in common? Just about nothing. When the opening bidder heard the one heart response, he was completely in the dark about responder's hand, outside of knowing it contained at least four hearts and at least six points.

BUT! 1 club — double. Partner's hand will usually be in the family of hands containing twelve to sixteen points with only one or two clubs. It also has, or should have, at least three cards in each of the unbid suits. Double will describe such a hand at least eighty percent of the time. It would be more than that except that occasionally you double with the intention of later bidding a suit to show a hand of substantial proportions, usually about 17 or more points.

Therefore, when a takeout double is made, the doubler will not be inclined to bid again. Only if the doubler has extra values will he take further action . . . . . unless . . . . . the responder makes a strength showing bid. Once a double has been made, the responder *must* bid the value of his hand. When he does, and the doubler can trust the responder to do so, then the partnership will be able to bid games when they should be bid. And they *won't* be going down when they push unnecessarily to the two or three level when someone overbids as a result of an imperfect system.

I cannot think of another area of bidding where so much is lost. More points are thrown away on hands involving takeout doubles than on any other.

True, the disasters may not always be spectacular, but there are so many of them that they add up, and up, and up, and . . . .

CHAPTER III   THE TAKEOUT DOUBLE

There is one last item to be covered in the area of takeout doubles and responding to them.

Having gotten this far with the discussion, can you begin to guess what this item is?

Well, so far, we have looked at responses to takeout doubles and how the doubler should proceed with the subsequent auction, if any. At this point, you should be well able to handle the bidding after the takeout double has been made.

The missing item then is the double itself. What should the doubler have? How many points does he need? What must his distribution be? What exceptions, if any, exist?

In the previous section, all the examples of doubles were reasonable. It was too soon to deal with unreasonable doubles as well as unreasonable responses to unreasonable doubles.

My feeling is that the double itself does not often lead to trouble. Usually, the resulting problems develop in the subsequent bidding. However, it is not the case that all the doubles ever made are proper, or even close to it.

Hardly!

While it is true that the poor results following a misjudged double are few, the size of the disaster can be quite impressive. These examples are typical, and while I hope you are not guilty of them, I can assure you they can and do occur.

North
♠ Q108764
♥ 3
♦ AK103
♣ J2

North	East	South	West
Pass	1♣	Dbl	1♥
4♠	Dbl	All Pass	

South
♠ 5
♥ KJ10
♦ Q974   This was down quite a few, which should have
♣ AQ1043   been no surprise. The double was terrible and
violated one of the prime rules of takeout doubles. A takeout double is for takeout, not for penalty, as the player here apparently intended. Double should show no more than two cards in the doubled suit. If South passes as he should over one club, the final contract will be either one notrump by South or two spades by North. Quite an improvement. A typical auction might be:

North	East	South	West
Pass	1♣	Pass	1♥
1♠	Pass	1NT	Pass
2♠	All Pass		

Better than 4♠ doubled?

North
♠ 3
♥ K108764
♦ 972
♣ K54

North	East	South	West
—	1♦	Dbl	4♦
4♥	Pass	4♠	All Pass

South
♠ AJ863
♥ 32
♦ 10
♣ AQ876

This time South was lucky. No one doubled. But South was down three, which was silly because three hearts would have made while four diamonds would have been down two. The actual result was quite poor, and quite unnecessary. This time South violated the rule of having support for all the unbid suits when making a takeout double.

North
♠ 3
♥ KJ873
♦ A932
♣ 1032

North	East	South	West
Pass	1♣	Dbl	2♣
3♥	Pass	3♠	Pass
4♦	Pass	Pass	Dbl
All Pass			

South
♠ Q107642
♥ 10
♦ KQ8
♣ A95

There are those people who would blame North for this result. Four diamonds was down three, or 500 points. At the table South said North should have bid only two hearts and that North should also subsequently pass South's two spade bid. This was South's suggested auction.

North	East	South	West
Pass	1♣	Dbl	2♣
2♥	Pass	2♠	All Pass

Unfortunately this auction violates a number of rules one must follow in order to have a successful partnership. The first rule is that a double followed by a new suit shows extra values, above those already shown by the takeout double. The second rule is the one covered at such length in the previous chapter: Responder must bid the full value of his hand. Here responder has a good hand.

North

♠ 3
♥ KJ873
♦ A932
♣ 1032

After 1♣ , Dbl, 2♣ ?, North's hand is worth almost twelve points, and the way to show this is to jump to three hearts, as was actually done. In fact, a jump to four hearts would be reasonable action. As you have seen, North should bid two hearts if his hand is much weaker:

North

♠ 32
♥ KJ873
♦ J943
♣ 107

Therefore, bidding only two hearts is quite an underbid with the actual hand.

North

♠ 3
♥ KJ873
♦ A932
♣ 1032

This, for repetition is the complete hand and the auction which ultimately led to the disaster.

South	North	East	South	West
♠ Q107642	Pass	1♣	Dbl	2♣
♥ 10	3♥	Pass	3♠	Pass
♦ KQ8	4♦	Pass	Pass	Dbl
♣ A95	All Pass			

The fault was clearly South's. If South just overcalls with one spade, the bidding will surely go no further than two spades by South. Possibly the opponents will play in two or three clubs. All these possibilities are better than the actual result.

Here is a list of what a takeout double should show and what it should not show.

A takeout double shows:

1. At least thirteen points in support of the unbid suits. If you have previously passed, a double may be shaded to eleven points in support of all the unbid suits.

2. At least three cards in each of the unbid suits.

3. No more than two cards in the suit doubled. On rare occasions one may have three cards in the suit doubled.

A takeout double should not be made when:

1. The hand has two suits.

2. The hand has only one suit, and there is no extra strength.

Here are some hands to practice your judgment. When the bidding has been opened on your right, what do you do, if anything, with the following hands?

♠ K1076	1♣	?	Double. This is a perfect, though minimum, double of an opening one club bid.
♥ A732			
♦ KQ95			
♣ 3			

♠ K8762	1♣	?	Double. Do not bid one spade.
♥ AQ93			
♦ Q54			
♣ 3			

♠ A76	1♥	?	Double. Some players guarantee four cards in
♥ 42			the other major when they double a major for
♦ KQ108			takeout. This practice is nice when it works, but
♣ A865			too many partscores and even games are lost

when that rule is followed too strongly. You would like a fourth spade here, but you just do not have it. So, if your hand warrants a takeout double, but has only three of the other major, go ahead, double anyway.

♠ 3	1♠	?	Pass. Even though you have enough points to
♥ Q74			make a takeout double, this hand has two flaws.
♦ KQ53			You have poor heart support, although that alone
♣ KJ953			should not stop you, but more importantly,

your partner will have to respond at the two level, if he chooses to bid a suit. Be aware of this when you are considering action over a one spade opening bid, as opposed to another suit. When your side has to bid at the two level, it means you will have to take eight tricks rather than the seven which your side would need at the one level. That extra trick can be crucial when partner has nothing and you get doubled in the bargain.

♠ 7	1♠	?	Double. Here you have support for each
♥ A1086			suit, so if partner selects one, you
♦ A982			will be assured of a decent fit. This is a
♣ K1098			minimum double of one spade.

♠ 3	1♠	?	Pass. This hand has exactly the high cards as the
♥ A642			previous hand. However, it does not have any
♦ A543			fillers. Missing are the tens and nines found in
♣ K752			the first hand. When you have a hand which

seems to suggest action of some sort, but which is minimum, your decision to act may often be resolved by the presence or lack of spot cards. Those tens and nines in the first hand may be worth nothing or they may be worth as much as one or even two extra tricks. I would guess their value at a full trick.

♠ A432	1♣	?	Double. Your partner can bid any suit at the
♥ K632			one level. You would not double a spade, had
♦ A873			that been your singleton (see previous hand), but
♣ 4			when the opening bid is one club, a double is fine.

♠ A1086	1♦	?	Pass. You have no support for hearts, and there
♥ 9			is no convenient way to get into the bidding now.
♦ KQ54			Best to pass and hope for a later opportunity to
♣ KJ73			do something.

♠ Q2	1♥	?	1NT. Do not double. That would show
♥ AQ3			better spades, and anyway, 1NT
♦ KQ54			shows this hand perfectly.
♣ A1062			

♠ 42	1♥	?	Pass. Not enough here for 1NT, and the
♥ K76			pattern is wrong for a double.
♦ AJ97			
♠ KQ108			

♠ KQ107	1♣	?	Double. If partner responds one heart or one
♥ AQ7			diamond, you will bid 1NT. This shows about
♦ Q107			16 to 18 in high card points. It is the same
♣ A108			hand which would overcall 1NT except that

it looked best to double first, looking for a fit. If partner can bid spades,
it will probably lead to a better contract than would be reached by a direct
1NT overcall.

♠ AJ1076	1♦	?	One spade. There is a long, long argument
♥ Q42			between two schools of players on
♦ 76⁻			these hands. One school says double
♣ AJ3			with this hand, and the other says

bid one spade. If you listened to both sides of the argument, you might be
listening for longer than you like. And when you got through listening, you
might still not feel you had the answer.

I suggest you take this approach, which I will not attempt to justify. When
you have a hand which is basically one suited, you should overcall almost all
of the time, if your suit is a *major* suit. If your suit is a minor suit, you should
double when *feasible*, otherwise overcall.

♠ 3	1♠	?	Double. Do not overcall. If you overcall,
♥ AJ7			you will never get to show the adequate
♦ K1065			support you have for the other suits.
♣ AQ865			Admittedly, if you double, you may lose the

club suit, but on the balance, double will be right at least twice as often as
the overcall.

Hand	Bid		
♠ K3	1♠	?	Two clubs. If you want to pass instead,
♥ Q2			I suppose that is all right. But there
♦ K107			is no way that a double is.
♣ AJ9876			

Hand	Bid		
♠ AJ7	1♥	?	Double. Your club suit is not too good
♥ 4			and given the reasonable alternative
♦ KQ10			of doubling, you should not be embarrassed
♣ Q76542			at all with either your spade or diamond support.

Hand	Bid		
♠ 742	1♥	?	Two clubs. You have exactly the same high
♥ 7			cards as the previous hand, but your
♦ KQ9			spade support is rather poor and
♣ AQJ1087			your club suit is especially strong.

As it is, I would not completely rule out a double, although I think that would be stretching things a bit.

Hand	Bid		
♠ Q87642	1♦	?	One spade. When your suit is a major, you
♥ AJ3			should tend towards bidding it, when your
♦ J			choice is between bidding or doubling.
♣ KQ10			

Hand	Bid		
♠ AQJ1087	1♦	?	Again one spade. What goes for the
♥ K107			previous hand goes even more strongly here.
♦ 4			
♣ QJ3			

Hand	Bid		
♠ KJ1087	1♦	?	One spade. This is the kind of hand which
♥ AQ654			can lead to very poor results if a
♦ 42			double is chosen. Should partner somehow find
♣ 7			a response in a major

suit, then well and good. But if he responds with two clubs, or some number of notrump, as you and I know he will do, what then? Well, what is going to happen is that you are going to pass two clubs, or whatever else partner bids, and it is going to be a filthy result.

Oh! Do you feel that if you got a two club response that you would bid two hearts or two spades? That is nice. Which one do you bid? And while you are wondering which suit to bid, answer this question.

1♦	Dbl	Pass	2♣
Pass	2♥		

How much does the two heart bid show? If you have done your homework, you will know that two hearts shows substantially more than the initial double promised. A typical hand might be:

```
♠ KJ7              ♠ AQ107
♥ AKQ1074   or    ♥ KQJ1084   etc.
♦ A7              ♦ 3
♣ J2              ♣ K3
```

It is clear that a double followed by a new suit shows about seventeen or so points. It is equally clear that the hand in question:

```
♠ KJ1087
♥ AQ654
♦ 42
♣ 7
```

cannot be bid in this way. Even the most pie-eyed optimist would not try to claim this is as fine a hand as either of the example hands. If things break badly, the problem's hand may produce remarkably few tricks. The example hands will seldom fail to produce six or seven tricks.

These hands are not at all alike in value or distribution. Therefore, if possible, they should not be bid alike. And as you have seen, it is possible to bid these hands differently and yet correctly. Just remember to ask yourself this question when you are considering a double as opposed to an overcall. "If I double, and subsequently bid a new suit, will my hand prove a disappointment to my partner?" Partners are notoriously more critical of your bidding than anyone else is, so if you can please them, then everything will be OK. And everything will be OK if you have the extra values your bidding requires.

```
♠ KJ10987     1♦    ?    One spade. You do not have enough
♥ AQ74                    to double and then bid spades.
♦ 42
♣ 10
```

```
♠ AKJ107      1♥    ?    One spade. You may later show the
♥ 42                     club suit if the bidding permits. Double here
♦ 10                     is wrong for all the above reasons. You do not
♣ K8642                  have enough to subsequently
```
bid a new suit should partner make his response in your short suit.

If you follow the rule of not doubling with two suited hands, you will be well ahead in the long run.

```
♠ AQJ1072     1♦    ?    One spade. This hand is actually strong
♥ 4                      enough to double first and then bid
♦ 7                      spades. The trouble with that would be
♣ AK875                  that you may not get a chance
```
to show the club suit. Partner might have some hand like this one:

♠ 4
♥ A87
♦ 8642
♣ 96432

This hand will probably produce four spades, but it will also produce six clubs. Only in the unlikely event that one spade is passed out will the simple overcall cause a poor result.

If you play strong jump overcalls, then an immediate two spade bid may well be best.

The significant point of this hand is that even with a hand as strong as this one, and even possibly with one stronger, an overcall will work out better than a double.

♠ KQ107	1♦	?	Double. Do not get too excited because of the
♥ A9876			void. If you do not have a decent fit, the limit
♦ —			of this hand may be a partscore, if even that.
♣ AQJ4			Do not make the mistake of cuebidding two
			diamonds.

♠ KQJ7	1♦	?	Double again. This hand is good enough to insist
♥ AJ1064			on a game only in the event that partner can bid
♦ ——			a suit. If he has nothing but a slew of diamonds,
♣ AK109			you will not be able to guarantee anything.

Notice that in both of these hands, a double will not get you too high when partner has a bust. If partner has some diamonds which he feels are good enough to make a penalty pass, then you should not object. Some players make cue bids on hands like these because "I did not want partner to pass one diamond doubled." But if partner does pass your double, you will probably defeat one diamond a few tricks, and more important, you will find you did not have a game of your own. After all, if your partner decides to pass the double, it means he has at least five diamonds, and probably more. That does not leave much room for him to have another suit. And if he does not have a suit to bid, then you *do not* have a fit.

One more point. You will remember from the discussion on responding to doubles that you pass only when you *expect* to set your opponents. If you do not expect to set them, you find a bid.

Remember this hand?

♠ 3
♥ 7642
♦ 1087642
♣ 73

If partner doubles one diamond, you would respond one heart. Even though you have six diamonds, you have no reason to think you can beat one diamond. Therefore you bid. This time you have four hearts. In some circumstances you would have to bid a three card suit.

♠ KQJ7   Going back to the actual hand, you will see that as long as
♥ AJ1064   you can trust your partner not to pass your double through
♦ —   fear alone, then that action will be best on almost all hands.
♣ AK109   Only when you have a strong two suiter or a strong one
suiter will it be right to cue bid.

♠ AK107   1♣   ?   Still double. If partner passes, do you think
♥ AKJ93   one club will make? If you trust partner, a double
♦ AK32   is right.
♣ —

♠ AKJ1097   1♦   ?   Two diamonds. This is the kind of hand you need
♥ AQJ86   to cue bid. If partner can bid hearts or spades
♦ —   by himself, you will give serious thoughts to a
♣ A3   slam. If he bids anything else, you will eventually
extract a preference from him for spades or hearts and will bid a game at least.

♠ AQJ10876   1♦   ?   Two diamonds again. You know you can make four
♥ AQ   spades, and there may easily be a slam. Should
♦ —   partner have, say, Axxxx of clubs, then seven
♣ KQJ9   clubs may be easy.

♠ AQ3   1♦   ?   Again a cue bid of two diamonds is
♥ KQJ10932   the right bid. You hope to find
♦ —   out if partner has the heart ace, the
♣ AK3   spade king, or even perhaps a good club suit.

     Whether to cue bid or to double? Cue bids should be used when you have a strong two suiter, and your main interest is in finding which suit partner prefers. Or, a cue bid should be used when you have a sufficiently strong one suiter to insure a game. Your partner will soon realize what kind of hand you have and will cooperate with you if he has anything to suggest there is a slam.

     Do not cue bid when you have 5-4-4-0 or 4-4-4-1 distributions. These hands will be better handled by a takeout double. After all, if partner bids a suit, you can still make a cue bid, and you will have left open the opportunity for partner to pass the double, should his hand so indicate.

CHAPTER IV   DIFFICULT HANDS

By now, if you have pursued this book in its order of presentation without skipping, you may well and reasonably be convinced there is nothing left to the topic of takeout doubles and responding to them. It is true that if you follow the preceding material faithfully, you will be well placed to handle most problems steming from takeout doubles. You will be using an excellent bidding structure which cannot help but contribute to the partnership harmony and rapport as trust in each other develops.

Therefore, all your problems are over. Yes? . . . Sadly . . . No.

Using the bidding methods so far described in the book will save you a lot of problems, but there will always be a number of hands which do not respond easily to "system." Problems you will have, some easier than others; some harder. There will be hands where you just know you should be doing something, but what should that "something" be?

This section will help you develop the basis needed for judgment in such situations. We are going to take a look at some of these problem hands and see what that "something" may be. Study these hands closely. The answers and the *reasons* for the answers should help you when similar situations come up at the table. And I promise you, they will come up.

I promise also that this will be the end of our discussion of takeout doubles.

Onward.

♠ A109   1♣   ?
♥ AQ2   Double. Your distribution is terrible, but you have
♦ 543   a bit extra in high cards. If you want to pass,
♣ KQ73   that is all right, but you probably will not be able
to take any later action. If you pass and your left hand opponent also passes, your partner may not have enough to re-open. Admittedly, you would like more cards in the major suits, but you do not have them. But you do have at least three. If partner jumps, you have enough high cards to take care of your "lack" of support.

♠ KQ7   1♣   ?   Double again. Here is a hand which breaks the
♥ AJ4   rule of having no more than three of the opponents'
♦ AQ9   suit. (Usually you should not even have three
♣ 5432   cards.) But you do have support for the unbid suits
and you do have extra values in the terms of high cards.

♠ A103   1♣   ?   One notrump. Do not go doubling when you have
♥ AK7   a clear descriptive bid available.
♦ A102
♣ J1062

♠ Q2   1♣   ?
♥ AQ106   Double. This hand is not exactly classic in terms
♦ KQ86   of distribution required for a takeout double, but
♣ AJ3   double is right. Overcalling one notrump is not
wrong, but it may rule out playing in hearts or diamonds. The reason that double is right is that if partner responds with one spade, you can rebid one notrump. This will tell your partner that you are not too thrilled about spades. It tells partner you have the strength to bid one notrump *directly* had you wished, and the reason you doubled first was that you had hearts and diamonds which you did not wish to bypass.

If by any chance, your partner jumps to two spades, you will be happy to bid three notrump, describing your hand almost perfectly. Partner probably will pass three notrump, but if he bids again, your hand should not be a disappointment to him.

♠ AQ107   1♦   ?
♥ 102   Double again. If partner bids one heart, you
♦ KQ9   can bid one notrump. The same reasons as in the
♣ AQ108   above hand apply here. Partner will know you
have spades since you went out of your way to double first. Remember that this auction shows the same values as the direct one notrump overcall.

♠ KQ10   1♦   ?   One notrump. Do not fall into the habit of bidding
♥ J2   too quickly. Nothing is gained by doubling.
♦ AQ107
♣ AJ97

♠ AJ102   1♦   ?
♥ 54   Do not double. Plan ahead. What will you do if
♦ AJ3   partner bids one heart? Pass? How will partner
♣ K954   like your dummy? He will not like it? Nor can
your bid one notrump if partner bids one heart, as that shows the values for a one notrump bid. And this hand is not that good.

The right bid here is pass. If you want to experiment, you might try overcalling one spade. Not perfect, but better than a double.

♠ AQ107   1♦   ?
♥ KQJ9   It is theoretically right to pass as you do not
♦ Q84   have any club support. However, if you want to
♣ 102   bid, and who does not want to bid, then you might
try a double on the theory that partner will try to respond in a major suit if he can. If he bids two clubs, he will probably have five of them and the result may not be too bad. Certainly double may lead to a good result. If, however, you go for 800 in two clubs doubled, you may blame me if you wish, but you will have to apologize to your partner. It is risky to double, but the gains will outweigh the losses.

♠ 102   1♦ ?   Pass. When you make light doubles, you must
♥ AQ107   have both major suits. You are not ready for
♦ Q84   a spade response from partner. Do not start
♣ KQJ9   something you cannot finish.

♠ Q862   1♦ ?
♥ AQ103   Pass. Much as you would like to bid, there is no
♦ A1095   clear cut action. You could try one heart, but
♣ 8   the dangers are significant. Certainly, it could
work, but in the long run pass will be best. Anyway, your hand will be quite
well suited to defend against anything except clubs. A good general point of
information is that hands with strength in the opened suit will frequently be
very useful for defense.

♠ KJ87   1♦ ?   Pass again. This hand is very much like the
♥ 4   previous one. But here, there is a good chance
♦ A1063   that you will be able to get into the auction safely
♣ KQJ4   at a later time. The bidding may well go this way.

1♦	Pass	1♥	Pass
2♥	?		

Now you can double. This is still a takeout double and your partner should
read it as such. He will know you have length in the two unbid suits and he
will know you are short in the suit you doubled and long in the suit originally
opened. In this case, partner will realize you have short hearts and long
diamonds.

If you did not have this distribution, you would have doubled the opening
bid and not waited. The fact that you did pass first, and then later found a
double implies a hand like the actual one.

♠ 7   1♣ ?   Pass. The same idea. If the bidding continues,
♥ A1063   1♣ Pass 1♠ Pass
♦ KJ96   2♠ ?   you can double, as in
♣ AK104   the previous hand. Partner will play you for length
in the red suits and he will know you did not double the round before
because you were short in spades and consequently long in clubs.

These delayed takeout doubles are not too common, but when they do
occur, they are very effective. Here are a couple of hands where the delayed
double worked to perfection.

Partner	Partner		You	
♠ 10643	Pass	1♣	Pass	1♠
♥ A8762	Pass	2♠	Dbl	Pass
♦ K3	4♥ !			
♣ 107				
You				
♠ 5				
♥ KQ103				
♦ AJ95				
♣ K982				

Here is a case of evaluating one's cards perfectly. Your partner, holding the North hand, dealt and passed. East opened with one club. You, South, passed. West responded one spade and East raised. Now South's hand, which had had no convenient bid earlier, can and did make a delayed takeout double. Now look at North's hand. Only seven points in high cards, but what sensational cards they are. North felt in fact that his hand was so good, it was worth a direct jump to game. And he was right. He made an overtrick. North thought along these lines.

"I have seven points in high cards, two useful doubletons, and a *fifth* heart. This hand is worth at least ten points and I am inclined to feel it is worth more than that. I'm going to bid four hearts rather than three because partner will have no way of knowing I have this much."

South, incidentally, should not make one of these delayed doubles without the values of an original double. The only thing that has changed is the distribution promised by an original double. Bear in mind that you will need a good hand to invite partner to bid at the two or three level, regardless of how the auction has gone to that point.

CHAPTER V PREFERENCE, OR THE FINE ART OF LETTING PARTNER PLAY THE HAND

In the course of many auctions you and your partner are going to be involved in a number of obligations. You will be telling him when possible, the strength of your hand, and he will be trying to tell you the strength of his. You will be involved in showing him what suits you hold and he will be showing you his suits. "Can a suit fit be established?" is one question the partnership must answer. "Should the hand be played in notrump?" is another. "Where are we going?" These are all important facets of bidding and they make up a large part of what bidding is all about.

Unfortunately, there comes a time when a tentative or even final decision must be made. Perhaps there is some reason that you cannot go further. The reason may be lack of a fit, or it may be lack of strength. But whatever the reason, the auction should stop. And the way the auction should stop is (frequently) in the form of a preference bid.

When a preference is given, it may well be the end of the bidding. Of course, on some hands, the bidding will continue. But when the auction *should* stop, and the preference is *not* given, then the auction may be forced onward to either the wrong level or the wrong suit or both.

Preferences are probably the most overlooked and underused bids in bridge. Here is how the preference bids work. A preference is an admission of having more cards in one of partner's two (or three) suits than in the others. *And* a preference implies no more strength than has already been shown.

These hands are intended to review all kinds of preferences. When is a preference a signoff? Is it meant to end the auction or does it have encouraging overtones? Can the preference be passed or is it a forcing bid? And more importantly, what is the potential danger if a preference bid which should be made is not made? See if you are not familiar with some of these situations and the ensuing results.

	You	Partner	
♠ 1076	1♦	1♠	Bid two spades. This is not a
♥ J87	1NT	2♥	raise of spades. The bid suggests
♦ AJ106	?		only that you have reason to believe
♣ AK9			that spades is a better trump suit than

hearts. When you rebid one notrump earlier you denied four spades, so 1076 is quite adequate for this auction. Partner will not be unhappy with your spade holding.

Incidentally, when the opening bidder rebids one notrump, a new suit by responder is not forcing. If the opener has this hand:

♠ 82
♥ J873
♦ AK107
♣ KQ3

and the auction goes as before, then the opener may pass. This is just about the only time a new suit by responder can be passed.

The auction:

	You	Partner
	1♦	1♠
	1NT	2♥
	2♠	

shows no more values than already shown by the one notrump rebid.

RULE: When a bid has been made to show a certain range of points, there is no ensuing bid which can change that range. Later bids can only describe additional bits of information within the already announced range.

	You	Partner
♠ Q107	—	1♠
♥ 42	2♣	2♦
♦ K87	?	
♣ AJ1042		

Two spades. This is a common sequence in which the preference shows a hand which is worth more than a direct raise to two spades and less than the forcing raise of three spades. The hand should be worth about ten to twelve points with three card spade support.

	You	Partner
♠ J97	—	1♠
♥ 4	2♣	2♥
♦ A1076	?	
♣ K10642		

Two spades again. Notice that there is no reason at all to suggest playing this hand in notrump. Almost always, if a good fit exists in a major suit, then you should play in that suit and not concern yourself with notrump.

	You	Partner
♠ 842		
♥ A10654	—	1♠
♦ AJ73	2♥	3♣
♣ 2	?	

Three spades. By all means, you must resist the urge to bid three notrump on the theory that all suits are stopped.

If you are concerned, incidentally, with the possibility that partner might pass three spades, ask yourself these questions:

1. How many points has partner shown by his three club bid? He has shown significant extra values inasmuch as he has forced the bidding to the three level. It is hard to define the values in terms of points, so I will describe them by way of examples.

Given the auction: 1♠ by you as opener, 2♥ by partner as responder, the following hands are strong enough for you as the opener to rebid 3♣ .

♠ AK1096	♠ KJ876	♠ AKQ107	♠ QJ1093	♠ J10864	♠ QJ10864
♥ 42	♥ 3	♥ ——	♥ 4	♥ A2	♥ ——
♦ 7	♦ KQ	♦ A32	♦ KJ3	♦ 43	♦ 5
♣ AQJ86	♣ AK1043	♣ K10964	♣ AKQ10	♣ AKQJ	♣ AKJ1063

Notice that all of these hands are stronger by far than a minimum opening bid. Either the distribution is good, or there is additional high card strenth, or the hand has both features, good distribution and extra strength.

Given the same starting auction: 1♠ by you as opener, 2♥ by partner as responder, the following hands are not worth a three club rebid by you the opener.

♠ QJ1073	2♠	Not enough high	♠ KQ876	3♥
♥ 4		cards to compensate	♥ A32	
♦ AQ		for the better	♦ 3	
♣ K6432		distribution.	♣ Q632	

♠ AKJ107	2♠		♠ Q10987	2♠
♥ 4			♥ K2	
♦ J73			♦ 103	
♣ K542			♣ AK109	

♠ AK1093	2♠
♥ A2	
♦ 9	
♣ 87654	

None of these hands have enough extra strength to warrant forcing the auction to the three level. Therefore, do not do so.

If you feel that by not rebidding three clubs, you may get a poor result because you lose a club fit, then I say it can happen. You may incur a poor result. But you will have many more poor results when you do have the hand necessary for the three club rebid, because partner will always have to guess if this time you have the extra values for your bid. Keep partner happy because your bids follow a system. A happy partner makes for a happy partnership.

Having ascertained that rebidding a new suit at the three level shows extra values, now answer question two.

2. What does responder's two over one show? Unless you are playing a rather unusual system, a two over one response should show some hand worth at least ten points.

Given the auction: 1♠ by partner as opener, 2♥ by you as responder, 3♣ by partner as opener, the combined hands should be worth in the neighborhood of twenty six or more points, assuming no one has cheated on his bids. Therefore, it is reasonable to say that when the bidding goes this way, you must continue to a game contract.

Repeating the hand given moments ago.

	You	Partner	
♠ 842	—	1♠	
♥ A10654	2♥	3♣	You should bid three spades,
♦ AJ73	?		knowing that partner will bid
♣ 2			either four spades, or three

notrump, or even perhaps he will make a slam try. If you fail to bid three spades here, and choose instead to bid three notrump, you will probably stop the auction. You will probably also be in an inferior contract. Not necessarily, but probably. If you bid three spades, your partner will still be able to make a decision. It is more important to tell him about the spade fit than the diamond stopper.

	You	Partner	
♠ Q103	—	1♠	
♥ KQ1054	2♥	3♣	Three spades. Knowing that this
♦ 432	?		is a forcing bid, you can allow
♣ KJ			partner to decide, for example, on

three notrump. You do not have a diamond stopper, but partner may, and from his side, three notrump may be a laydown. In any case, whatever partner does will be OK. Do not make decisions when your partner is better placed to decide than you are.

	You	Partner	
♠ 1087	—	1♠	
♥ 753	2♦	3♣	
♦ AKQ7	?		Three spades, expecting partner
♣ A102			to be able to make the best final

decision. It is on hands like this, where it is necessary for you to have a good partnership agreement. As far as you are concerned, three notrump or four spades could be right. If you and partner can trust each other to the extent that three spades is forcing in this sequence, then you can make that bid with confidence, knowing partner will make the final decision. True, he may not make the right choice all the time, but he will be right more often than you because he will have more information to work with in deciding where to place the final contract.

Judgment Situations

So far, the preference situations discussed have been of a systemic nature rather than of a judgment nature. Judgment situations are different. Partner has bid two or more suits and you have to decide whether to:
1. Rebid your suit again.
2. Show your other suit, if you have one.
3. Bid some number of notrump.
4. Give preference to one of partner's suits.
5. Pass.

These preference possibilities have one thing in common. Whatever you do, it may end the auction. You are no longer involved in constructive bidding as was the case in the previous section. Instead you are concerned with ending the bidding in as playable a contract as possible. In fact, on occasion, your goal will be to reach as "un-bad" a contract as possible. You may realize that nothing can make and your concern is to stop the bidding before someone wises up to your problems and says "Double!"

This is the typical format for disaster:

North
♠ KJ1076
♥ QJ842
♦ 93
♣ 2

South
♠ 3
♥ 10
♦ AQ8764
♣ KQ743

North	East	South	West
Pass	Pass	1♦	Pass
1♠	Pass	2♣	Pass
2♥	Pass	3♣	Pass
3♥	Dbl	4♣	Dbl
4♦	Pass	Pass	Dbl
All Pass			

After this has gone for some unbelievably large number, the recriminations start. In the actual auction here, South is really innocent of anything wrong. North on the other hand is guilty of two terrible calls. The fact that North is all to blame for the final contract does not stop him from expressing his opinion of the disaster. If he cannot complain about the bidding, he will have something to say about the dummy play. South on the other hand was so disgusted with the dummy that his subsequent play was affected by his emotion and was deserving of North's criticism. Wonderful. Just the thing to tune up a partnership. How do you think this pair will perform for the next hand, and the one after that? Do you think their rapport will be helped by this debacle? No way!

How should the bidding have gone? Much faster!

North

♠ KJ1076	North	East	South	West
♥ QJ842	Pass	Pass	1♦	Pass
♦ 93	1♠	Pass	2♣	Pass
♣ 2	2♦ !			

South   END

♠ 3
♥ 10
♦ AQ8764
♣ KQ743

To continue bidding with North's hand is an open invitation to calamity. Sure you may have some chance of game in hearts, or even spades. But if hearts is right for you, you will have to bid them and then *rebid* them in order to play in hearts. Remember, partner is going to bid over two hearts. Now what happens when partner does not like hearts or spades? What happens is that you have pushed the bidding up to the three or four level on a misfit hand. What happens now? Well, you go down. The only question is how many do you go down. And if you get doubled, well . . . Unlucky? No. Sad? Yes. Could it be avoided? For sure.

Let us look at some more examples and see how a bit of judgment in potentially dangerous situations can turn large minuses into small minuses or even small pluses.

	Partner	You
♠ K10987	1♦	1♠
♥ Q9742	2♣	?
♦ 42		
♣ 3		

This is of course the same hand you faced a moment ago leading up to this discussion. The

correct bid here is a simple two diamonds. **RULE: When faced with a misfit, stop the bidding as soon as reasonably possible.**

	Partner	You
♠ AQ1096	1♦	1♠
♥ KJ842	2♣	?
♦ 73		
♣ 3		

This hand has sufficient values to try two hearts. If partner bids two notrump, you should pass. If

partner goes back to two spades, you can *try* for a game in spades, although a pass is probably right. If partner bids three clubs, you will go back to three diamonds, *not* three hearts. When a misfit appears, use the rule and stop the bidding. The reason you can bid two hearts is that you have enough high cards to justify the bid. Distribution does not necessarily mean you have to bid. If partner bids three notrump over your two heart bid, you should pass! Do not make the mistake of trying four hearts. Partner will not have three spades and most of the time he will have only one or two hearts. You have shown pretty much what you have and partner said "Three notrump is the spot." The addition of the fifth heart should not give you cause to override him. **RULE: When your bidding has reasonably described your hand, and partner then makes a decision, trust him. You must have a strong reason to override him.**

	Partner	You
♠ AJ10964	1♦	1♠
♥ QJ1082	2♣	2♥
♦ 3	3NT	?
♣ 7		

This time it is correct to bid four hearts. Both of your suits are playable opposite poor support and you have six-five distribution, which is significantly better oriented to a suit contract than five-five distribution is.

	Partner	You
♠ Q86432	1♦	1♠
♥ A9654	2♣	2♥
♦ Q	3NT	?
♣ 10		

Pass. True you have six-five shape, but your suits are terrible. That diamond queen and even the club ten will be pleasant surprises to your partner, who will no doubt congratulate you on a well-judged pass.

	Partner	You
♠ KJ876	1♦	1♠
♥ A842	2♣	?
♦ 3		
♣ 765		

Pass. Two clubs may not be ideal, but it is likely to be a better spot than any of the other contracts you may end up in if you bid again.

Remember that two hearts by you now is forcing and will probably lead to a three level contract. Is this hand worth it?

	Partner	You
♠ A8642	1♦	1♠
♥ Q10873	2♣	?
♦ 4		
♣ 107		

Well? It is hands like these that cause accidents. I would not blame anyone for bidding two hearts, but if it works out poorly, do not be surprised. In practice, it will probably be better to pass and hope for the best. Believe it or not, you have some chances of good things happening here. The opponent on your left may have a few hearts himself and may try two hearts, hoping his partner has a few. As you can see, his partner will not have hearts.

	Partner	You
♠ QJ9876	1♦	1♠
♥ 10764	2♣	?
♦ 82		
♣ K		

It is not always necessary to take a preference. Here you can rebid two spades with the expectancy that it will be at least as good a contract as two diamonds. Partner is expected to pass this bid of course and will do so unless he has a good reason not to pass. (His reasons for bidding over your signoff bid will be discussed shortly.)

	Partner	You
♠ QJ10864	1♦	1♠	Time to give up. Bid three diamonds.
♥ A42	2♣	2♠	Partner will not be unhappy with
♦ 432	3♣	?	your hand. It includes an ace,
♣ 3			three trumps, and a singleton.

This hand, in fact, is really quite excellent and you are entitled to be unhappy if partner cannot make three diamonds.

	Partner	You
♠ Q965432	1♦	1♠	Three diamonds. You have expressed
♥ K76	2♣	2♠	strong interest in playing spades,
♦ J2	3♣	?	and your partner has gone back
♣ 7			to his suits anyway. Humor him.

You cannot return the auction to two spades, which is probably the correct contract. In any case, partner has good reasons for removing two spades to three clubs (remember, he is on your side) and you should go along with them. Your diamond support is quite good enough considering you have already tried to avoid them.

	Partner	You
♠ Q86542	1♦	1♠	Two diamonds. Your hand is too
♥ K1063	2♣	?	bad to want to hear any more bids
♦ J2			from partner and two diamonds has
♣ 7			a good chance to end the auction.

If you wanted to try two spades, that is not too bad, but the rule is that when faced with a misfit, you should get out early. Under no circumstances should you try two hearts or two notrump with this hand.

	You	Partner
♠ 876	1♦	1♠	Two spades. This is not a raise
♥ 10	2♣	2♥	*of* spades. It is a preference
♦ AQ1053	?		*to* spades. All partner knows is that
♣ AK98			you prefer spades to hearts

and you thought a preference was better than bidding notrump or rebidding one of your own suits.

A preference is really sort of a neutral bid. If nothing else, it tends to carry quite a few negative inferences. A player who makes a preference bid denies the ability to do something constructive. Usually then, when your partner gives a preference, his hand will be some sort of minimum for his previous bidding.

The above hand is quite nice for the auction so far. If partner makes any move toward game, you will accept gladly and confidently.

	You	Partner
♠ Q2	1♥	1♠
♥ AJ876	2♣	2♦
♦ 3	?	
♣ AJ943		

Well? You have all suits stopped. How many notrumps will it be? Hopefully, it will not be notrump at all,

but will be a two spade call. True, you have only two spades, but a doubleton queen is adequate for this auction. This is a least of evils bid. You could bid three clubs, but partner might have to pass and if he has only two clubs, it will not be fun playing there. Or, he may go back to three hearts, in which case you will wish you had bid two hearts instead of three clubs. At least then you would be a trick lower. But this is just an endless circle really, because if you choose instead to bid two hearts, it may go all pass. If partner has only one heart, and there is no reason for him to have more, two hearts will prove quite inadequate as a home. Bidding two spades on the other hand will almost always lead to as playable a spot as you have on this hand and it has the advantage of keeping the bidding low.

Incidentally, do not worry about the possibility that partner has not got five spades. If he has four only, he should not be bidding in this fashion.

	You	Partner
♠ 4	1♥	1♠
♥ KQ1097	2♣	2♦
♦ J8		
♣ AQ432		

Sometimes you just cannot give a preference, assuming you would like to. Here your best bid is two hearts, which has the advantage

of avoiding the three level. Only if partner bids again will you have to go higher. Partner probably will pass unless he has extra values, or unless he clearly prefers clubs in which case he will return to clubs.

	You	Partner
♠ 4	1♦	1♠
♥ 103	2♣	2♥
♦ AQJ87	?	
♣ KQ1042		

Here again, you cannot take a preference so you must choose a rebid of some sort. Three clubs is best assuming you do

not bid two notrump. As long as you are rebidding a suit, choose the most descriptive one, which is clubs in this case. That will show five-five distribution at least and denies the inclination to try any number of notrump instead.

	You	Partner
♠ J2	1♥	1♠
♥ AJ987	2♣	2♦
♦ Q2	?	
♣ AQ54		

Finally, a two notrump rebid. You have a hand which for a change does not suggest a misfit and its values consist of adequate high

cards rather than distribution. You have a mild fit for both of partner's suits so that notrump will play adequately as a contract.

	You	Partner
♠ Q	1♦	1♠	Two notrump. You might bid three
♥ K9	2♣	2♥	clubs but you do have sufficient
♦ KQJ108	?		high cards to bid notrump and your
♣ QJ752			high cards in the major suits

will be helpful for both of partner's suits.

	You	Partner
♠ 72	1♦	1♠	This is the sort of hand on which you want
♥ J3	2♣	2♥	to bid three notrump. You have all
♦ AKQJ10	?		suits stopped and you have a
♣ A1087			reasonable shot at nine tricks

almost any time partner has a decent minimum. On the same auction as this, you might bid three notrump on either of these hands:

♠ Q   ♠ 8
♥ J2   or   ♥ J54
♦ KQJ107   ♦ AQ1087
♣ AQJ96   ♣ AKQJ

	You	Partner
♠ 8	1♦	1♠	Pass. Two spades is a signoff
♥ Q84	2♣	2♠	bid. Partner may have as many as
♦ AQ652	?		ten points but usually it will
♣ KQ82			be less. Something like this

hand is the average:

♠ KJ9762
♥ K43
♦ 92
♣ 107

As you can see, two spades is as good a spot as you can find. Two notrump by you will get you too high. Clearly, if partner's bidding is to be trusted, you should give no thought at all to bidding beyond two spades.

	You	Partner
♠ Q83	1♦	1♥	Pass, again. Partner has signed
♥ ——	2♣	2♥	off. Admittedly, clubs or
♦ AJ964	?		diamonds may be a better spot,
♣ AJ642			but passing will work out

best in the long run. Bear in mind that looking for a better spot requires going to the three level. And what is to stop partner from bidding *three* hearts? Best stop while it is cheap.

	You	Partner
♠ ———	1♦	1♠
♥ 42	2♣	2♠
♦ AQJ1083	?	
♣ KQJ97		

Three clubs. To be sure, there are hands where you may override partner's signoff and this is one of them. Here you know that clubs or diamonds will be best and you need only to know which one it is. In the previous hand, your suits had no quality and it would be no thrill to play in three diamonds with ♦ AJ964 opposite ♦ 72. However, ♦ AQJ1083 opposite ♦ 72, is more than adequate. It is the good quality of your suits that gives you cause to run, not the fact that you have five of each and no support for partner.

Of course, partner may still rebid his suit, but that is life. At least your effort to look for a better contract, for once, was justified.

	You	Partner
♠ 3	1♦	1♠
♥ KQ7	2♣	2♠
♦ KQJ108	?	
♣ AQ64		

It might well be right to pass, but you do have an awfully good hand. It is this fact that gives you license to bid two notrump.

This bid is strong and highly invitational. It is *not* an effort to get out of spades. If you had a bad hand, you would pass, or if you had to, you would rebid one of your suits. As you saw just a few hands ago, you just do not run from a signoff bid unless you have a good reason.

	Partner	You
♠ J109864	1♦	1♠
♥ K83	2♣	2♠
♦ K2	2NT	?
♣ J3		

Three notrump. Partner has said he is interested in a game in spite of your weak bidding. He is definitely not trying to get out of spades for the sake of getting out of spades. If partner is interested in a game, so should you be with this hand. You have the king of diamonds, which partner will love dearly, and you have the jack of clubs which should also be quite valuable. Everything you have is going to fit in nicely with partner's hand. The thing to avoid is bidding three spades. That would sound weak, relative to your previous bidding, when in fact, you have a very good hand within its announced limits.

	Partner	You
♠ QJ87654	1♦	1♠
♥ Q74	2♣	2♠
♦ 2	2NT	?
♣ 63		

Here is what a return to three spades should look like. You know partner is looking for a game but you have no reason

to encourage him. This hand has little to recommend notrump and your suit is quite good enough to play opposite a singleton. You may not make three spades, but you surely were not going to make two notrump.

	You	Partner	
♠ Q3	1♥	1♠	This hand should strike you by
♥ AQJ76	2♣	2♠	now as being quite satisfactory
♦ 3	?		for spades, so you should not
♣ AK1042			consider looking for a better

suit. In fact, this hand is so good that it is probably worth a raise to three spades. Partner will be able to judge his hand quite accurately and he will go to game with most any hand which will offer a play for it. He will bid four spades with:

♠ KJ10762	♠ AJ106542	♠ J109864
♥ K	♥ 3	♥ K2
♦ 8642	♦ 1076	♦ K1086
♣ 93	♣ J5	♣ 3

There will be no guarantee that four spades will make with these hands, but it will be a makeable contract more often than not.

Partner will pass three spades holding:

♠ KJ8642	♠ 10976542
♥ 4	♥ 2
♦ Q83	♦ QJ3
♣ 753	♣ Q3

Partner's decision will be based on the quality of his spade suit, and he will tend to rate highly cards he may have in hearts and clubs while discounting cards in diamonds.

	You	Partner	
♠ AJ764	1♠	2♦	Pass. By now you should have
♥ K10732	2♥	3♦	no trouble giving up on these hands.
♦ 2	?		Partner has at least six or more
♣ A4			diamonds and you have two

bad suits and a minimum at that. Let it go while you can.

	You	Partner	
♠ AKJ108	1♠	2♦	This is the kind of hand you need
♥ AQJ104	2♥	3♦	to keep bidding in the face of a
♦ 42	?		signoff. You have two good suits,
♣ 9			either of which may produce a

game if partner can help. Here you bid three hearts not because you are afraid of three diamonds, but because you still have reasonable expectations for the hand. In the previous hand, you could hope only to find a better partscore. In this hand you hope to find a game. Quite a difference.

	You	Partner	
♠ AJ10654	1♠	2♣	Again, it is very reasonable to
♥ A109432	2♥	3♣	persevere with three hearts. Even
♦ Q	?		though your high cards are minimal,
♣ ———			your distribution is superb.

Game is not at all out of the question. You may end up going for a number, but the risk is worthwhile and should be taken.

Unfortunately, most players when given this hand bid three hearts, but for the wrong reasons. They are bidding in an effort to escape from partner's club suit. This is wrong! Remember the rule again. When faced with a misfit, give it up as soon as possible. If you keep on bidding, you should have a *constructive* reason for doing so, and merely trying to find a good partscore does not qualify as a constructive reason. You need a reasonable chance for game to continue on with misfits.

The reason so many bad results crop up in this area is that each player has incurred disasters like this one.

North
♠ 42
♥ J3
♦ AK9643
♣ 1052

South
♠ AQ9865
♥ AQ64
♦ ———
♣ Q63

South	North	
1♠	1NT	Someone doubled and the
2♠	3♦	result was quite unsatisfactory.
3♥	4♦	Where did the auction go wrong?

It is possible to criticize the two spade rebid, but it is not the worst bid in the world. As it is, two spades would have made. The trouble began when North tried three diamonds. Had he held no spades at all, the bid might have been excused. But holding two of them, the run to three diamonds is unbelievable. After all, how many spades did South expect North to have? At this juncture, South should have passed and taken his chances. But he did bid three hearts. Perhaps he had seen North's bidding before this. North now had the chance to go back to three spades, but for some reason, rebid his diamonds. South finally got the message and gave up. Watching the play of his hand was no treat for South. When he discovered his partner had not just one spade, but two, there began a lecture of unbridled proportions. Anyone who has sat as dummy through one of these debacles does not need to be reminded of the anguish, and anyone who has not so suffered should be spared.

It is enough to say that the partnership was somewhat unnerved when this one came along.

North
♠ J
♥ Q10
♦ KJ1087
♣ A10975

South
♠ Q108765
♥ KJ964
♦ A
♣ K

South	North	
1♠	2♦	North might have passed three
2♥	2NT	hearts, but holding good intermediate
3♥	3NT	spots his choice of three notrump
4♠	5♥	was not far out of line.

South on the other hand has a clear pass after three notrump. His partner knew he had at least five-five in hearts and spades and he still wanted to play three notrump. South, holding cards in both minors, and also holding a reasonable opening bid in terms of high cards, should have said pass. But, logic aside, and memories of the earlier disaster still fresh in hand, South carried on, hoping, or probably expecting, to find some as yet unknown spade support in partner's hand. After all, if North can hide support once, can't he do it again? Probably yes, but this was not the time. At this point, North should have passed, but for some reason, he decided at long last to give a preference. Wrong again. Four spades would have made as it turned out. Five hearts did not.

The preference to five hearts of course was quite misjudged, as South was known to have more spades than hearts. But remembering the lecture he had just received, or perhaps some parts of it, the preference was duly given by North, and the result was duly bad. Very sad. Would you like to bet on this pair's chances to do well next time?

The reason so much time has been devoted to these two hands is, as before, to show you what effect a bad result may have on subsequent hands. If the partnership is not working well, or worse, not working at all, or worse yet, if the partners are working at odds with each other, then there is no confidence, no rapport, and consequently distrust, disharmony, and lousy results.

When you learn how to give up on a misfit hand, and when partner knows you know, and you in turn know partner knows, your results on misfits will improve immensely.

You probably will not notice the good results, because they are small and unassuming. What will be noticed is that you are not going for an occasional bundle when someone persevered with a misfit. As they say, out of sight, out of mind. But when you are talking about poor results, out of sight is best.

CHAPTER VI   MORE DOUBLE TROUBLE
Bidding After Opponent's Takeout Double

Earlier, we had a rather long discussion on how to handle takeout doubles and responding to them. I promised that there would be no more discussion of this topic. Well, there will not be. This section is not going to deal at all with what you need to double your opponents. Instead, it is going to deal with what to do when the opponents double *you*.

When you open one club, get doubled, and your partner responds one heart, can you answer these questions?

1. How many hearts does partner guarantee?

        Four_____   More than four_____

2. How many points does he guarantee?

        6 to 9_____   Less than 6_____   Unlimited_____

3. Is partner's one heart bid forcing?

        Yes_____   No_____

There is a lot to be said for each of the various understandings possible. Some people play that a new suit over a takeout double should be weak and nonforcing. These people feel that if they do not bid, the double may be passed for penalty: 1♣ — Dbl — Pass — Pass — Pass. They would like to be able to bid one spade over the double on some hand like this:

> ♠ QJ874
> ♥ 1083
> ♦ 10976
> ♣ 3

Others like to redouble automatically on all hands containing ten or more high cards points. The theory here is that when they bid, instead of redoubling, partner will know whether or not a game can exist because a bid categorically denies ten points. These hands would all bid as indicated over a double of partner's opening one club bid:

♠ AJ10864		♠ 10		♠ 3		♠ 42	
♥ K1065	1♠	♥ A42	1♦	♥ AJ965	1♥	♥ QJ86	1♦
♦ 42		♦ QJ10642		♦ K10642		♦ K6542	
♣ 3		♣ 863		♣ J4		♣ 32	

On the other hand, these hands would all redouble:

♠ 3	♠ J9765	♠ AK107	♠ KQ10865	♠ 4	♠ AQ109
♥ AQ10642	♥ 3	♥ 54	♥ 3	♥ 53	♥ KJ87
♦ KJ97	♦ AKQ10	♦ 8	♦ 107	♦ AK1065	♦ Q964
♣ Q3	♣ J42	♣ K96543	♣ AQ32	♣ KJ842	♣ 3

These approaches work quite nicely when they work, but when they do not, look out! What can go wrong, you say?

Let's say partner bids one diamond, and it is doubled.

If you redouble, what do you do when the bidding proceeds:

	Partner		You	
♠ J9642	1♦	Dbl	Rdbl	2♥
♥ 3	?	4♥	?	
♦ AQ107				
♣ K54				

Do you double? Your hand is quite unsuited to defense because of your length in diamonds. Do you bid four spades and then complain when partner has only one or two spades? Or do you bid five diamonds and then discover that four spades is the correct contract? Or lastly, do you pass, expecting partner to bid? What is he going to bid? How can he tell? All he knows is that you have ten points. But where these ten points are or what they consist of, he has no clue.

How about this hand.

North	North		South	
♠ 42	1♣	Dbl	Rdbl	When this hand was played, West
♥ K1064				jumped to four spades over South's
♦ 42				redouble. When this was passed to
♣ AKQ87				South, what was he to do?
South				
♠ 10				
♥ AJ7532				
♦ KQ63				
♣ 53				

As you can see, five hearts can be made, but who should bid it? South did double four spades and it made. Clearly this was not the best result possible.

Obviously, it would be nice if there were some way to avoid mishaps like these. It turns out that there is a reasonable way to handle almost all hands without getting into trouble. Here it is.

A redouble still shows ten or more points, *but,* a new suit at the one level does not *deny* ten points. You may in fact have a very good hand, and still bid a new suit at the one level. The reason for this is that when you redouble, aggressive opponents may be able to jam the bidding, making it difficult for you to show your suit. This suggests that whenever you have a good hand with one or two suits, you should begin by bidding them, regardless of your strength. This means that a new suit at the one level is forcing.

On the other hand, a redouble will now show one of three hands.
1. A hand intending to raise partner.
2. A hand intending to bid some number of notrump.

3. A hand hoping to double the opponents.

Using the above guidelines, try to decide on your bid on each of these hands.

	Partner		You
♠ KJ1087	1♣	Dbl	?
♥ 4			
♦ A103			
♣ Q976			

Bid one spade. If you redouble, you may have trouble both showing your spades and your club support. This bid guarantees no more than it would if there were no double. Partner will not treat it as more than six points. On the other hand, he will not pass. You will get another opportunity to describe your hand, if you wish.

	Partner		You
♠ KQJ7	1♣	Dbl	?
♥ 42			
♦ J1076			
♣ 1097			

One spade again. You will not expect to take another bid. If there were no double, you would also bid one spade not expecting to bid again.

	Partner		You
♠ QJ987	1♦	Dbl	?
♥ K4			
♦ 542			
♣ 1076			

One spade. Same reasoning as above.

	Partner		You
♠ 109852	1♥	Dbl	?
♥ 3			
♦ AJ842			
♣ J7			

One spade. You would bid one spade if East passed. If you would not mind bidding after a pass by East, you should not mind bidding just because he doubled.

	Partner		You
♠ Q1076	1♥	Dbl	?
♥ J2			
♦ K76			
♣ 8642			

Pass. Without East's double, you would respond one spade or one notrump. After East's bid, you should not wish to bid with minimum values. After all, no one says you *have* to bid.

	Partner		You
♠ J976	1♦	Dbl	?
♥ K104			
♦ 102			
♣ KJ87			

One notrump. Your spade suit is too poor to bother with, but your hand is good enough to bid something.

	Partner		You
♠ 98642	1♦	Dbl	?
♥ K4			
♦ 1073			
♣ AJ2			

One spade. A five card major suit should be bid if you decide to bid at all.

	Partner		You
♠ 3	1♣	Dbl	?
♥ KQ1086			
♦ AQ542			
♣ 103			

One heart. In spite of your opening bid, you do not redouble. This hand shows why you should play the one heart bid as forcing. At your next turn, you will jump in diamonds if possible. Partner will know you have two good suits with an opening bid or even more. If you redouble, you might not get the opportunity to show both suits.

	Partner		You
♠ 10	1♦	Dbl	?
♥ AQ8642			
♦ K1086			
♣ Q3			

One heart again. If you redouble, you may not be able to show your hearts and your good diamond support. From your point of view, you may be able to make a slam in either red suit (hearts or diamonds). Maybe three notrump is best. Perhaps there is no game available at all. If you redouble here, partner will know only that you have ten or more points. But if the opponents have a fit and can jack up the auction quickly, it may turn out that partner will not be able to use the information that you have ten points. Frequently he would rather know whether you have support or a suit of your own.

One way of looking at this is as follows. The difference between a bid and a redouble is about four points. A minimum bid shows about six points and a minimum redouble about ten. If you choose to bid rather than to redouble, you will have a good chance to show your values later, while accurately describing any important distributional features now.

On the other hand, if you must redouble after a one club opening and a double on your right with:

♠ A864		♠ KQ108764		♠ K10864
♥ K107	or	♥ AQ73	or	♥ ———
♦ KJ32		♦ J2		♦ AQ2
♣ 42		♣ ———		♣ Q8642

then your subsequent problems will frequently be insoluble.

	Partner		You
♠ J842	1♣	Dbl	?
♥ K1076			
♦ AQ3			
♣ 42			

Here is a nice minimum redouble. The opponents will not be able to bid too gaily here because you will be able to double them.

There is *no way* the opponents can embarrass you in the auction.

	Partner		You
♠ QJ76	1♠	Dbl	?

Redouble. Do not make the common mistake of jumping to three spades. After a double, a jump raise is pre-emptive. It denies much in the way of high cards and promises good support with reasonable distribution. A jump to three spades here would *not* be forcing. Do you want the auction to die in three spades?

♥ A1064
♦ 3
♣ K976

	Partner		You
♠ 97642	1♥	Dbl	?

Three hearts. This is the sort of hand you need to make a jump raise after a double. You have good trump, good distribution, and not much in high cards. Notice that you do not consider bidding one spade. That would be in violation of one of the most important and effective rules of bridge. **RULE: When partner opens in a *major* suit, and you have good support for him, (four cards) and you know that his suit should be trump, *do not* get involved in other directions. Bid in such a way as to show that you intend to play in his suit while describing your points at the same time.**

♥ A963
♦ 2
♣ J107

You have no intention of playing the above hand in spades. You intend to play in hearts. So bid the maximum number of hearts your hand allows, which in this case is three.

Consider also that it will be much harder for the next player to bid over three hearts than over one spade.

One last suggestion here. I have seen some players try to be cute by passing and then later raising hearts. Don't! All that happens is that the opponents have more room to bid and your partner has no chance to do anything at all because he will have no idea what you have.

	Partner		You
♠ 42	1♠	Dbl	?
♥ AJ87			
♦ K107			
♣ AQ97			

Another easy redouble. You will either double the opponents or you will continue to three notrump.

	Partner		You
♠ AJ3	1♥	Dbl	?
♥ 107			
♦ KJ103			
♣ K642			

Redouble again. You will not have any trouble later describing this hand.

	Partner	You
♠ Q1076	1♠	Dbl	?
♥ 4		
♦ 103		
♣ AJ9872		

Four spades. You expect to make it but you do not wish to give the opponents room to find their fit, and as you see, they probably have a good save somewhere. Do not bid only three spades.

	Partner	You
♠ A543	1♥	Dbl	?
♥ KQ1073		
♦ 2		
♣ Q32		

Redouble. You will eventually go to four hearts. Do not bid only three hearts now as it might get passed out. Four hearts now is a reasonable tactical bid as it may keep the opponents from saving. But if you do bid four hearts, and it goes five diamonds on your left, pass, pass, to you, what will you do? Partner's pass will have been based on the idea that you have a bad hand and it is clear you will have misled him. So your bid here will be somewhat of a guess.

If you redouble first and they later take a save, your partner will be able to contribute to the final decision. It might go:

Partner		You	
1♥	Dbl	Rdbl	3♦
Pass	4♦	4♥	5♦
?			

Your partner now can double, which you will pass, or he can bid five hearts knowing you have a good hand. He will have a better idea of your hand than you of his. Or he can pass, which means he is unsure of the best action and wants you to have the last say. You will double or you will bid five hearts. All this may seem a bit strange, but it is quite logical.

Throughout these hands you should not lose sight of the fact that when you redouble, you will be able to handle the subsequent auction, barring unforeseeable circumstances.

You may have noticed that only bids at the one level are forcing over a takeout double. If you have wondered about that, as well you might, I will try to explain why. There are three reasons.

One. Bidding at the two level takes up more bidding room than responding at the one level. The bidding room lost makes it very difficult for you to make the fine distinctions between hands that is available when you can respond at the one level.

Two. You cannot have a new suit at the two level be both forcing and possibly weak at the same time. You will not have room to handle the later bidding. Therefore, the bid must be either, forcing with at least ten points, or non-forcing with less than ten points.

Experience has shown that you will have about three times as many hands of the five to nine point range than the ten or more range. You should, then, play two level responses after a double as non-forcing to cater to the greater number of situations.

Three. One tends to play new suits at the two level as non-forcing because they will generally be made in a minor suit. You are less likely to have a minor suit game so it is less important to make this a constructive auction. When is the last time the auction began

| 1♥ | Dbl | 2♣ | or |
| 1♠ | Dbl | 2♦ | |

and you eventually arrived at a game?

If all this is confusing in theory, it should be less so in practice.

	Partner	You	
♠ 42	1♥	Dbl	?
♥ 7			
♦ KQ10963			
♣ Q542			

Two diamonds. This shows a good suit, but not enough to redouble. This hand is about average.

	Partner	You	
♠ 52	1♠	Dbl	?
♥ 7			
♦ K10984			
♣ A10876			

Two diamonds. You intend to try three clubs later. Partner will know you did not redouble so you are limited to less than ten points.

Hopefully, partner will not hang you for taking two bids on this hand. He should not.

	Partner	You	
♠ 4	1♠	Dbl	?
♥ 432			
♦ AJ109842			
♣ 76			

Two diamonds. This is not even quite a minimum. This may be the last chance to show your diamonds.

Once in a while, you do have a good hand that does not fall into any of the established categories for redoubling. Sometimes you can solve the problem by jumping in a new suit: 1♥, Dbl, 3♦. This shows a good six card suit and about ten points. It is not a forcing bid.

And sometimes you have a hand for which there is no answer. When this happens, what do you do? Well, you improvise by choosing the bid which *least* distorts the bidding. Try to make a little lie rather than a big lie.

	Partner		You
♠ 72	1♦	Dbl	?
♥ 1063			
♦ 42			
♣ AKQJ86			

Three clubs. Partner may pass, but if he has the right hand, he is welcome to try three notrump or whatever else his hand calls for.

	Partner		You
♠ 3	1♥	Dbl	?
♥ 107			
♦ A86			
♣ KQ107432			

Three clubs. This bid does not guarantee a solid suit. It merely shows a good six card suit (or longer) and a reasonable hand.

	Partner		You
♠ 764	1♥	Dbl	?
♥ 3			
♦ AQJ1062			
♣ J107			

Only two diamonds. You are just short of a jump to three diamonds.

	Partner		You
♠ 3	1♠	Dbl	?
♥ QJ10842			
♦ AJ87			
♣ J2			

Three hearts. Your suit is not quite as good as you would like, but partner may be able to bid four hearts which is game.

It is the possibility of a ten trick game rather than an eleven trick game (clubs or diamonds) which makes this bid reasonable.

	Partner		You
♠ 42	1♥	Dbl	?
♥ 7			
♦ AKQ1076			
♣ K1042			

Well? This is one of those problem hands, if you are following the outline so far described. Two diamonds and three diamonds are both non-forcing and are underbids. Redouble is chosen here in spite of the fact that the opponents' bidding may make you wish you had shown your suit instead. If you redouble, you will probably get to show your suit. If you do not get to show the diamond suit and you get to some terrible contract, you will be entitled to wish you were using some other system. But when the rest of your problem hands get handled nicely and efficiently, they should be noted. Keep score and see how this structure of bidding works out in the long run.

	Partner		You
♠ 107	1♦	Dbl	?
♥ KJ98			
♦ 4			
♣ AKJ864			

Another very difficult hand. I would redouble and hope for the best. If the opponents can pre-empt in spades, you may have to do some good guessing, but no solution here seems to look better than another.

	Partner	You	
♠ 42	1♦	Dbl	?
♥ KQ864			
♦ 3			
♣ AQ542			

One heart. This is forcing. You will likely get to show the clubs later. Notice that most problems arise when you have a good hand with a *lower* ranking suit than the one partner opened.

In practice, you will find you do not often have more than ten high card points when partner opens and the next player doubles. And of those instances, you will seldom have a hand with total emphasis on a suit or suits lower ranking than partner's suit(s). Usually you will be able to redouble or you will have a suit to bid at the one level, which is forcing of course.

Here are a few hands with no emphasis on any area. Try them out. If you have problems, look back at the preceding section.

	Partner	You	
♠ KJ874	1♣	Dbl	?
♥ Q2			
♦ 10742			
♣ Q7			

One spade. This is forcing for one round. You will probably pass partner's rebid although you would be happy to bid again if he makes a strong bid such as three spades.

	Partner	You	
♠ AK52	1♥	Dbl	?
♥ 10642			
♦ 73			
♣ 1083			

Two hearts. When you have four card support for partner's major suit, you should almost always raise to whatever level your hand indicates. Do not confuse the issue with one spade. Partner has hearts. You have hearts. Therefore you should play in hearts.

	Partner	You	
♠ K107	1♦	Dbl	?
♥ Q986			
♦ 42			
♣ A1063			

One notrump. This is just short of a redouble. It would not be wrong to bid one heart, but you would prefer a slightly better suit.

Having only a four card suit should not of itself be a detriment to bidding it, but it is reasonable not to rush to bid it.

	Partner	You	
♠ 43	1♠	Dbl	?
♥ 103			
♦ Q762			
♣ KQJ83			

Two clubs. You could try one notrump instead, but if the opponents compete in hearts, you would like to have partner lead a club. Furthermore, if he can raise clubs, you may well be able to outbid the opponents.

	Partner	You
♠ 83	1♠ Dbl	?
♥ 4		
♦ AKQ73		
♣ KJ932		

This is one of those difficult hands where redoubling may lead to problems. If the opponents can bid to three hearts before you can show your suits, you may miss your best spot. However, you cannot use any other method to show your suits now because you have no way to make a *forcing* bid in a suit lower ranking than the opening bid. Redouble is the least of evils here because it guarantees you will have a chance to bid again. Remember that a jump to three diamonds, or three clubs, shows a good six card suit and is not forcing.

	Partner	You
♠ 4	1♣ Dbl	?
♥ A96		
♦ 8643		
♣ K10963		

Three clubs. This shows a hand worth less than a redouble. You have excellent club support and you have good distribution. Hopefully this bid will make it difficult for your opponents to compete. Or, if they do, your bid will make it easy for partner to bid on or to double should his hand warrant it. If the bidding should continue this way:

Partner	You	
1♣	Dbl	3♣ 4♠
Pass	Pass	?

you must not make the mistake of bidding five clubs. Your three club bid told partner what you have. He has elected to defend against four spades.

You on the other hand have no idea what he has, so you have no reason to bid on. If you do choose to bid five clubs, it is the same as telling partner that he does not know what he is doing. It may be true that he does not know, and five clubs may well be the winning bid, but it is not a partnership bid. You will not find a good partnership bidding in this fashion.

	Partner	You
♠ 72	1♦ Dbl	?
♥ AK108		
♦ J3		
♣ 76432		

One heart. If there had been no double, you would have been quite happy to bid one heart. You have a good four card suit and adequate values. Do not make the error of passing. Likewise, do not bid two clubs. The suit is not worth mentioning. Now and then, you may miss a club contract, but if you do not bid one heart now, you will always lose the heart suit. You lose also the chance to get partner off to the best lead should the opponents buy the contract. After all, do you want a club lead?

	Partner		You
♠ KQ1097	1♣	Dbl	?
♥ AJ983			
♦ 4			
♣ J2			

One spade. When possible, it is usually best to start bidding suits. You have plenty to redouble, but it sometimes becomes difficult to describe your distribution.

	Partner		You
♠ J8765	1♥	Dbl	?
♥ Q1084			
♦ K63			
♣ 7			

Three hearts. This shows four trumps, good distribution, and less than a redouble in value. Do not bid one spade. When you know you have a major suit fit, tell partner.

	Partner		You
♠ 10763	1♣	Dbl	?
♥ 8642			
♦ AJ			
♣ J73			

Pass. Not enough to do much of anything. Your suits are bad and your values do not compensate.

	Partner		You
♠ 4	1♠	Dbl	?
♥ AQ10873			
♦ 87			
♣ 10642			

Two hearts. This is not forcing, showing a decent suit of five or more cards, and less than ten points.

	Partner		You
♠ AQ962	1♦	Dbl	?
♥ KQ74			
♦ 3			
♣ J92			

Redouble. The reason for not bidding one spade is that you have no fear of the opponents. Whatever they bid, you will be happy to double. They are not going to appreciate the result of this hand. Remember, when you have enough strength to redouble, you do so if you will be in a position to handle any subsequent bidding. Here, you are well able to do so. The only question is the size of the penalty you expect to incur.

	Partner		You
♠ KJ8	1♠	Dbl	?
♥ 42			
♦ AQ97			
♣ 10654			

Redouble. You intend to support spades later. You do not bid three spades now because it shows four spades, and not nearly as much in high cards.

In the other extreme, when you do support spades after the redouble, you do so without jumping:

Partner		You	
1♠	Dbl	Rdbl	2♥
Pass	Pass	2♠	

In this sample auction you are showing ten to twelve points in support of spades, which is what the hand is worth. The redouble has already shown ten points, so there is no need to jump later unless you have rather more than a minimum redouble, say thirteen or more points.

	Partner		You	
♠ J10874	1♣	Dbl	?	One spade. Do not rush to
♥ 4				support a minor suit when you
♦ 102				have a major suit available.
♣ AJ863				

	Partner		You	
♠ KQ7	1♠	Dbl	?	Two spades. It is better to
♥ J97642				show the fit than to try an
♦ 106				experimental two hearts. Partner
♣ J3				will pass, or at least he should

pass, if he has any of these hands.

♠ AJ842	♠ 1086542	♠ AJ1093
♥ 8	♥ K	♥ 103
♦ KJ53	♦ AK7	♦ A84
♣ Q92	♣ A54	♣ K106

Spades will be at least as good as hearts in any of these hands.

	Partner		You	
♠ 3	1♥	Dbl	?	Three clubs. This is the hand
♥ 106				with a good six card suit in
♦ K1076				neighborhood of ten points. It
♣ AQJ976				is invitational but not forcing.

	Partner		You	
♠ 107	1♥	Dbl	?	This is a nice raise to two
♥ AQ3				hearts. Do not hide good support
♦ 42				for partner's major suits unless
♣ J109762				you have good reasons. Six clubs

to the J109 is not a good enough reason.

	Partner	You
♠ 82	1♣ Dbl	?
♥ 1063		
♦ K43		
♣ QJ1082		

Two clubs is enough. The club holding is quite good enough for a jump to three clubs, but the distribution is bad and the strength is minimum. If the diamond king were the ace instead, it would be a minimum three club bid.

	Partner	You
♠ K108	1♥ Dbl	?
♥ 10		
♦ KJ83		
♣ A7632		

Redouble. You can handle the subsequent bidding easily. If the opponents bid clubs or diamonds, you can double, and if they bid spades, you can bid notrump. If the opponents bid two or more spades, you can double that. The rule again is: Do not redouble unless you can handle most of the likely subsequent auction.

Most of the possible exceptions to this rule have been covered in the discussion or in the example hands.

Rebids by the Opener

If you decide to play this style of bidding after an opponent's takeout double, you have to make one or two slight changes in the rebidding considerations of the opening bidder.

These changes, if any, are not really very serious. Remember:
1. If partner responds at the one level in a new suit after a takeout double, you *must* bid again if your right hand opponent has not bid in the meantime.
2. If partner has bid *anything* else, including a redouble, you are not compelled to rebid. You may pass should your hand so indicate.

These examples should cover most of the possible rebidding situations that may occur.

	You	Partner
♠ K107	1♣ Dbl	1♥ Pass
♥ 42	?	
♦ KQ5		
♣ AJ763		

Partner's one heart bid is forcing and you must bid again. You would have bid one notrump quite happily had the bidding gone without competition, so you should choose that bid here. One notrump. In general, you should make the rebid you would have made in an uncontested auction. Only occasionally should your rebid be influenced by the opponent's double.

	You	Partner
♠ 9642	1♣ Dbl	1♠ Pass
♥ K7	?	
♦ K82		
♣ AQ107		

Two spades. Your opening bid is minimum, but you must still find a rebid. Partner may have a good hand and game is not at all impossible, in spite of your light opener.

	You		Partner	
♠ Q97	1♣	Dbl	1♠	Pass
♥ 432	?			
♦ A65				
♣ AKJ2				

Normally you might rebid one notrump, but here, your partner's spade suit is almost surely, a very good four cards, or even more likely, five cards. Raise to two spades.

	You		Partner	
♠ 872	1♣	Dbl	1♠	Pass
♥ K54	?			
♦ A65				
♣ AK107				

One notrump. Raising to two spades is not something you should go out of your way to do. In the previous hand, you were afraid of the heart suit, and your spades were headed by an honor. This hand is significantly different. All suits are stopped and the spades are bad.

	You		Partner	
♠ J87	1♦	Dbl	1♠	Pass
♥ 42	?			
♦ AKJ76				
♣ A104				

With this hand, it could be right to rebid two diamonds or two spades. One notrump is out because of the weakness in hearts. Here I choose two spades. Partner probably has a good spade suit because he bid it after a double. On the balance it is right to raise partner with these hands. In fact, it might be right to raise with worse spades than these, say 1072.

	You		Partner	
♠ 1087	1♦	Dbl	1♠	Pass
♥ 4	?			
♦ AJ973				
♣ AK54				

It is probably right to raise spades, even as bad as they are. If you want to bid two clubs instead, that is all right too. Do not make the mistake of passing though, that is not allowed.

Remember: Partner's bid of a new suit at the one level is absolutely forcing for one round.

	You		Partner	
♠ 1063	1♦	Dbl	1♠	Pass
♥ 2	?			
♦ AKJ1076				
♣ KJ4				

Much as I like to raise partner, this hand just does not quite make it. The diamonds are too good to suppress in favor of the poor (but barely adequate) spade support. Two diamonds here is best, although I have a sneaking admiration for anyone who wants to bid two spades.

	You		Partner		
♠ Q2	1♥	Dbl	1NT	Pass	Pass. This is the only one
♥ KJ863	?				level response which can be
♦ A107					passed. You have a balanced
♣ K103					hand and nothing extra.

	You		Partner		
♠ AQ7	1♥	Dbl	1NT	Pass	Raise to two notrump. Partner
♥ J10765	?				should refrain from bidding one
♦ 42					notrump with a minimum six points.
♣ AKQ					Game is not at all out of the

question if he has nine or even a good eight points. Partner will have the
advantage of knowing where the opponents' high cards are. As you saw in an
earlier chapter, it pays to bid aggressive games in these circumstances.
Knowing that most of the strength is in the doubler's hand should help
partner find the best line of play.

	You		Partner		
♠ K87	1♥	Dbl	2♣	Pass	Pass. You are no longer obligated
♥ AQ1096	?				to rebid after a two level
♦ K863					response. You have a minimum hand
♣ 10					opposite what is known to be less

than ten points. It is possible there is a better partscore contract than two
clubs, but you should not try to find it. If you do insist on looking for another
spot, you should try two hearts or two diamonds. Whatever you do, do not
bid two notrump. That bid would express an interest in game in light of
partner's two club bid. Two notrump here says, "I am interested in a game
even though I know you have less than ten points. Do you have a maximum
for your bid? If so, bid three notrump. Otherwise, pass or rebid your clubs."

	You		Partner		
♠ AJ862	1♠	Dbl	2♣	Pass	Again it is probably right to pass.
♥ 98642	?				Two hearts here is an acceptable
♦ AQ					choice however. The hand was
♣ 3					included in this section to impress

on you the strong consideration you should give to passing with hands in this
family. There is clearly no game, only a partscore. In such circumstances it is
frequently best to give up. Perhaps the opponents will bid again. *They* might
even try hearts.

	You		Partner		
♠ 98654	1♠	Dbl	2♥	Pass	A clear cut pass. No other
♥ 2	?				choice.
♦ AKJ					
♣ KQ76					

	You	Partner	
♠ A62	1♥	Dbl	2♣

Pass — Three clubs. This is quite a good hand and you might even raise to four clubs. Game is not at all out of the question.

♠ A62
♥ Q10654
♦ 3
♣ AQ62

If partner has as little as

♠ K87
♥ 3
♦ J54
♣ K108754

then five clubs can make.

	You	Partner	
♠ 8	1♥	Dbl	2♣

Pass — Three clubs again. Do not make the mistake of passing or bidding two diamonds. You are perfectly happy with clubs so there is no reason to give partner the idea that you do not like them.

♠ 8
♥ A10864
♦ KQ54
♣ K103

As for raising clubs or merely passing, the raise gets the nod. This follows the general rule that you should raise partner whenever possible. If you can make a game, then raising will help you get there. If the opponents compete, partner will be able to judge whether or not to bid on, to concede, or possibly to double. Lastly, if you raise, the opponents may not be able to compete. The doubler will have to bid at the three level should you raise, whereas he can bid at the two level should you pass.

	You	Partner	
♠ KJ876	1♠	Dbl	2♠

Pass — Pass. The raise to two spades here shows no more than a raise without the double.

♠ KJ876
♥ 107
♦ KQ9
♣ A54

	You	Partner	
♠ 43	1♥	Dbl	3♥

Pass — Pass again. A jump raise after a double denies a strong hand. It is pre-emptive in nature, showing less than ten points.

♠ 43
♥ AJ876
♦ K1086
♣ A10

Had there been no double, the 3♥ bid would be forcing to game.

	You	Partner	
♠ J9864	1♠ Dbl	3♣	Pass
♥ AQ10	?		
♦ KJ7			
♣ K3			

Three notrump. Partner's bid shows about ten points with a good suit. Your club king should give you a shot at six tricks in clubs alone. Partner's hand will look something like this:

♠ 7
♥ 962
♦ A96
♣ AJ10865

Even though the combined high card count is only twenty three points, you are a heavy favorite to make three notrump.

	You	Partner	
♠ AQ632	1♠ Dbl	3♣	Pass
♥ KJ74	?		
♦ A86			
♣ 2			

You should pass. Even though your hand has fourteen points, as did the previous one, you have no help for partner's suit. Best to pass and hope three clubs will make.

	You	Partner	
♠ KQJ86	1♠ Dbl	3♣	Pass
♥ AQ109	?		
♦ KQ3			
♣ 4			

Three notrump. The high cards and texture will hopefully make up for the lack of a fit for partner's clubs.

	You	Partner	
♠ A10765	1♠ Dbl	3♣	Pass
♥ KQ842	?		
♦ Q10			
♣ 3			

Pass. Your side has a misfit and the values for game are almost surely missing. It is possible that four hearts may make, but you will go minus too many times in looking for four hearts to justify the few times that it will succeed.

	You	Partner	
♠ KJ1087	1♠ Dbl	3♣	Pass
♥ AKQ94	?		
♦ 3			
♣ Q9			

Three hearts. This time you have extra values in the form of good suits and extra high cards. The added chance of a game justifies the risk of trying for it.

	You		Partner		
♠ 3	1♥	Dbl	3♣	Pass	Four or five clubs, depending
♥ Q10874	?				on your mood. There should be
♦ AK72					a decent play for five clubs. If
♣ K86					partner can bid five over four,

it should be cold, or close to it.

	You		Partner		
♠ AK7642	1♠	Dbl	3♣	Pass	A perfect fit! Bid four
♥ A3	?				notrump. If partner has an
♦ 2					ace, bid six clubs. If he has
♣ K753					both aces, bid seven clubs.

Do not make the error of rebidding spades or raising clubs. You know where this hand is going. Get it there. Do not make partner guess when you have a sure thing.

	You		Partner		
♠ KJ1076	1♠	Dbl	3♣	Pass	This one is tough. I would
♥ 542	?				try three diamonds, hoping
♦ AKQ					partner can bid three spades or
♣ AJ					three notrump. Three diamonds

will get your side to three notrump if partner has a heart stopper. This bid is not guaranteed however, and if three diamonds works out poorly, it will not be a surprise. But then no bid here looks flawless. Hopefully three diamonds will be the least evil choice.

	You		Partner		
♠ AQ1083	1♠	Dbl	2♣	Pass	Two notrump. Remember the
♥ AQ2	?				discussion from a few pages
♦ K103					earlier? This bid shows a good
♣ J2					hand and it invites partner

to bid a game if his hand is maximum for the range it has *already* shown. Two notrump is not a weak bid. It is not a sign-off. If the opening bidder has a weak hand with no fit, he *passes* the two club response. He does not bid two notrump.

When someone has a long suit in a weak hand, it is almost always best to play in the suit. Only if partner has an excellent hand or a fit for the long suit should three notrump be considered.

CHAPTER VII   FINE ART OF JUDGMENT

The bidding has gone in the following manner:

You			
1♣	1♥	1♠	2♥
Pass	3♥	Pass	4♥

This is a reasonably typical auction with an average amount of competitive bidding. The overcaller made a game try when he bid three hearts and the responder accepted the invitation. This time however, four hearts was too high, and even though no one doubled, it was two down.

Here is the hand that came down in dummy.

♠ J765
♥ Q54
♦ Q2
♣ KJ86

Do you remember the auction? Here it is again.

You			Dummy
1♣	1♥	1♠	2♥
Pass	3♥	Pass	4♥

There was nothing unusual in the play. The trump suit divided normally and the overcaller did in fact have a suitable hand to try for game. What went wrong in the auction? Responder certainly has a sound raise to two hearts. It includes nine high card points, good trump, and a possible ruffing value. In fact, when the hand was played out and the result established, the dummy was quick to point out the correctness of his bidding. "I had ten points and a doubleton", stated dummy, agitatedly, (he counts as well as he bids) "so you must have bid too much again and you should have played it differently, etc, etc."

Declarer, who could count, pointed out that the dummy had only nine points in addition to the doubleton, and then made the first pertinent comment of this, by now, quite heated discussion. "You had the wrong cards." This was not what dummy wanted to hear, so he formed another rebuttal and pursued. Let's leave them alone while declarer, tries, correctly, though possibly futilely, to convince dummy that four hearts was a bad bid and why.

Declarer's comment that "You had the wrong cards" is an application of the wonderful world of judgment, or if you prefer, evaluation, or even again, re-evaluation. It exactly sums up what went wrong in the auction now being discussed.

"You had the wrong cards." What does this mean? What is a "wrong card"? On the other hand, what is a "right card"?

Simply, a wrong card is one which the auction suggests will have less than normal value, perhaps even no value at all. A right card is one which the auction suggests will have more than normal value. Sometimes this increase in value can be enormous indeed.

Here are two extreme examples. In both cases, the bidding goes one club on your left, six spades by partner (!) and pass on your right. You have these two hands.

♠ KQ   ♠ 54
♥ 5432   ♥ 8765
♦ 76   ♦ 97
♣ 106542   ♣ KQ862

What is the value of the king and queen of spades in the first hand, and the king and queen of clubs in the second?

In the first case, you have a hand of unbelievable value. Partner over there has said he can make six spades, regardless of your hand. He does not have the king and queen of spades, and he still thinks six spades will make. His hand? It should be something like one of these:

♠ AJ1087654   ♠ A108765432
♥ A   or   ♥ ———
♦ AKQ10   ♦ AKQ
♣ ———   ♣ A

You may not agree with six spades, but it is clear that if partner can bid six, all by himself, you can bid seven and expect to make it.

The value of the king and queen of spades? Five points? More? How can you hope to put a price on them?

The king and queen of clubs, on the other hand, are of no value at all opposite either of partner's possible hands. They are together worth exactly zero. Nothing. They might as well not exist for all the good they are doing. The difference between the two hands can hardly be measured. One hand does nothing, while the other hand makes a grand slam possible. All kings and queens are not created equal.

This is surely an extreme example. But the points made are certainly valid and they can be applied to a large percentage of the bidding decisions you may have to make. Here is a short list of guidelines for judging the value of cards, along with some common exceptions.

1. Cards in suits bid by your partner (or shown by a takeout double) increase in value.

2. Kings increase in value when:

   a. The suit has been bid on your right.

   b. Most of the outstanding high cards rate to be on your right.

c. Partner has bid notrump.

3. Kings decrease in value when:

    a. The suit has been bid on your left.

    b. Most of the outstanding strength seems to be on your left.

    c. Partner is known to be extremely short in the suit.

4. Queens and jacks go up in value when partner has bid the suit or has bid notrump.

5. Queens and jacks go down in value when they are in suits bid by either opponent. If the suit has been bid on your left, they decrease more than had the suit been bid on your right.

6. Aces are always useful. If partner bids the suit, they are likely to be worth more than if the opponents bid the suit, but the increase or decrease is far less than in the case of lower ranking honor cards. Only when partner has a void is your ace likely to depreciate significantly.

7. Cards in unbid suits are worth more than cards in suits bid by the opponents.

Quiz

In order to help appreciate how evaluation works, try this quiz.

1. The bidding starts:

Partner		You	
1♣	1♥	?	Which is the better hand to have and why?

(1) ♠ A732　　(2) ♠ J732
    ♥ J76　　　　　♥ Q76
    ♦ K54　　　　　♦ K54
    ♣ Q32　　　　　♣ A32

The first hand is far better for you to hold in view of the auction. Only the heart jack is of dubious value. In the second hand, both the spade jack and the heart queen are questionable.

2. You hold the same hands. This time the bidding is:

	Partner		You
1♣	1♠	Pass	?

In this case, the second hand is much stronger than the first. Every card has some potential, whereas the club queen may be worthless in the first hand.

3. The bidding:

Partner	Opponent	You	Opponent
1♠	2♣	2♠	3♣
3♠	Pass	?	

Should you bid four spades on either hand?

(1) ♠ J76	(2) ♠ 8542
♥ Q854	♥ AJ953
♦ QJ63	♦ 762
♣ QJ	♣ 8

The first hand will be lucky to make just three spades. All those queens are deceptive. This is not really much of a hand. The club cards in particular are worthless.

The second hand, however, with four fewer high card points is not an unreasonable four spade bid. The fourth trump is quite valuable and the singleton club should be useful. The heart jack is in combination with the heart ace. It is worth more than it would be if the ace were not there.

4. The bidding:

You	Opponent	Partner	Opponent
1♥	1NT	Pass	Pass

Here are some opening hands. Do you like any of them after the bidding?

(1) ♠ KJ2	(2) ♠ AQJ	(3) ♠ KQ105
♥ KJ876	♥ KJ1082	♥ AJ10983
♦ AJ2	♦ K876	♦ ———
♣ Q2	♣ 3	♣ QJ10

The first hand with fifteen points is a death trap. Rebidding is begging disaster. Most of the missing high cards are sitting over you and your finesses are doomed to failure, assuming you can get to dummy to try them.

The second hand has fewer high cards but improved distribution. Partner will not need too much to make a successful partscore possible.

The third hand has such good distribution and such good spot cards that a game is still not completely out of the question. You should be very aware of the strength those tens and nines add to the hand.

5. The bidding:

Partner		You	
1♣	1♥	1♠	2♥
2♠	Pass	?	

Are any of these hands worth trying for game?

♠ J5432	♠ J86542	♠ A8765
♥ KQ7	♥ 3	♥ 9642
♦ Q95	♦ 7	♦ 3
♣ Q3	♣ A10654	♣ K102

You should pass the first hand. Those heart honors are probably opposite a singleton. This hand is worth little more than five or six points.

The second hand should not make a game try. You should bid game directly. Once a fit has been established, your hand significantly goes up in value. Here you have two fine fits, in both spades and clubs.

The third hand is clearly worth a try, if not a direct shot at game. Your heart length is an asset here, as it suggests partner has a singleton. If partner has as little as

♠ K1092
♥ 3
♦ K62
♣ AJ543

it may be possible to make an overtrick in four spades.

6. Again, which hand would you rather have when the bidding goes as indicated?

You	Partner
1♥	2♠
3♥	4NT
5♦	6♥

♠ K2	♠ 92
♥ AQJ1087	♥ Q108765
♦ 10762	♦ AKQ
♣ 3	♣ Q3

The first hand is much the better. The spade king is a wonderful card to have after partner's jump shift and the trump suit is better than it has to be.

The second hand has a number of flaws. The spade holding is poor and the trumps could be better. Even though it has thirteen points, this is not a good hand in terms of the auction. Partner does not seem worried about diamonds. Probably he has a singleton, which would mean your king and queen are unnecessary values.

7. As the bidding goes on, you will be called on to make various decisions. Should you try for game, for slam, or should you pass or double? Perhaps you have decided on a game level contract for sure but which one will it be?

The answer to these questions must always be based on the information available. This information comes from the previous auction, your hand, and your judgment.

If someone asked you "Do you bid four spades on?"

♠ J3
♥ 432
♦ AKQJ87
♣ 103

you would of course ask to know the auction to the point of the decision. Then, when you are deciding whether to bid or pass, you will have to answer this question, "Is this a good, average, or bad hand, in light of the auction to this point?" Sometimes you will find yourself loving a four point hand whereas a twenty point hand may suddenly become a death trap.

In the next group of hands, you should first look at the hand and form an impression of its worth. Then look at the bidding and then reappraise your hand. Do you like it more or less than before?

♠ K1076	You		Partner	
♥ A2	1NT		3♠	
♦ KQ102	4♣		4♦	
♣ A54				

This hand begins as a nice sixteen point one notrump. When partner jumps in spades, it becomes worth a four club cue bid. Partner's four diamond cue bid makes your hand look so good that a grand slam is not at all out of the question.

♠ KQ42	You		Partner	
♥ J2	1NT	2♠	3♥	Dbl
♦ KJ94				
♣ AQ3				

What started out as a normal and undistinguished one notrump bid has suddenly turned into a potential disaster. You have poor trump support and it looks like they are not going to divide very nicely.

♠ ———	You		Partner	
♥ 52	1♦	Pass	1♠	2♥
♦ AJ8765	3♣	Pass	3♠	Pass
♣ KQJ82				

At this stage you should give up and hope no one doubles. The point is that what was originally a hopeful hand has gone downhill. Expectations have gone to zero.

♠ 3	You		Partner
♥ AK6542	1♥	Pass	2♣
♦ 5			
♣ K8765			

Immediate ectasy! One of the nicest things of all is for partner to raise your suit or to bid a suit you like.

♠ A10876	You		Partner
♥ QJ942	1♠	Pass	2NT
♦ ———			
♣ KJ3			

This is almost as nice. You surely have a fit somewhere, perhaps spades, perhaps hearts. If partner had responded with two diamonds, you would be a bit leery.

♠ ———	You		Partner
♥ A108652	1♥	Pass	1♠
♦ A63			
♣ KJ32			

Your first impression here should be one of apprehension. Misfits are always nervous affairs and for the time being this may be one. If the bidding continues

You	Partner
1♥	1♠
2♥	2♠

then you should retire from the auction and hope that nothing bad happens. On the other hand, if the bidding continues

You	Partner
1♥	1♠
2♥	3♣

then your hand which seconds ago appeared to be going nowhere, suddenly looks like a star.

♠ Q1072
♥ AK10542
♦ 10
♣ K10

You		Partner	
1♥	Pass	2♦	Pass
2♥	Pass	3♣	Pass

This looks like another misfit and at this point you should be feeling cautious. If the bidding continues

You	Partner
1♥	2♦
2♥	3♣
3NT	4♥

then optimism is again justified. You should not be at all surprised to make a slam. Partner has gone out of his way to tell you he has a singleton spade with heart support as well. Come to think of it, you probably should bid a slam in spite of having only twelve points. Try Blackwood and see what happens.

♠ J7
♥ KQ975
♦ A1092
♣ 103

You		Partner	
Pass	Pass	1♣	Pass
1♥	Pass	1♠	Pass
1NT	Pass	2NT	Pass

This is an easy three notrump bid. The hand is a maximum in terms of what it has *already* shown.

♠ 76
♥ Q107
♦ Q10754
♣ AKJ

You		Partner	
1♦	Pass	1♠	Pass
1NT	Pass	2NT	Pass

This hand warrants no thought at all. Having opened the bidding, which many players would not do, you have nothing extra. There is no excuse for continuing on. This hand is a minimum for the range of values already announced.

♠ Q107	You		Partner	
♥ J2	Pass	Pass	2NT	Pass
♦ KJ432				
♣ 1063				

You should be quite happy with this hand. Three notrump will be a breeze. Bid it. Partner has about twenty two points with cards in all suits. He will be quite pleased with this dummy. You should be pleased to put it down.

♠ 42	You		Partner	
♥ KJ754	Pass	1♦	2♣	2♥
♦ K10642	Pass	3♦	3♠	Dbl
♣ 3				

You have seven high card points, but your partner is not going to be very happy to see them. Incidentally, you should pass three spades doubled. Do not bid three notrump.

♠ J1076	You		Partner	
♥ 72	Pass	Pass	1♣	1♦
♦ Q1042	Pass	Pass	Dbl	1♠
♣ J107	Pass	Pass	Dbl	Pass
	1NT	Pass	2NT	Pass

Believe it or not, you have a good hand! You should go on. In terms of what you have already shown, which is very little, you have a mountain. You did not bid over one diamond, and then passed again over one spade. Considering how much less you could have, you should bid three notrump and not be surprised if you make an overtrick.

♠ 92	You		Partner	
♥ AKQ10	1♣	1♦	Pass	Pass
♦ K3	Dbl	1♠	Pass	Pass
♣ AKQ82	Dbl	Pass	1NT	Pass

This of course is the reciprocal hand of the preceding problem. As fine as your hand is, you should not make the error of jumping directly to game. If you can trust your partner, and vice-versa, two notrump will be enough. Partner has twice denied having much. After your invitation, he will go to game if he can find any excuse whatsoever.

♠ J65	You		Partner	
♥ Q2	—	—	1♠	2♣
♦ 1087652	Pass	Pass	Dbl	Pass
♣ 94	2♦	Pass	2♥	Pass
	2♠	Pass	3♠	Pass

Once again, your hand has become a gold mine. You did not bid over two clubs, then merely took a preference to two spades, and partner is still interested in a game. "Do you have anything at all?" Well, you do. You have J65 of trumps. You might have had only two small ones. And you have the Q2 of hearts. That queen is a lovely card which partner will very much appreciate.

8. The questions in this section are to help your hand evaluation. For each of the hands given, construct three auctions which will show the hand in three different lights. One auction should make the hand appear quite nice, one should make it appear ordinary, and one should make the hand appear very unattractive.

Obviously, there are many possible sequences which fit the criteria. Some possible solutions are given but they include only a few of the available "correct" solutions.

If you just take the time and effort to do this part of the quiz conscientiously, your card appreciation and therefore your judgment will improve.

   A Auction which makes the hand quite good.
   B Auction which makes the hand seem ordinary.
   C Auction which makes the hand seem unattractive.

A. ♠ K1076	You		Partner	
♥ A94	Pass	Pass	1♠	Pass
♦ 42	2♠	Pass	3♥	Pass
♣ J876				

Your good hearts and spades make this hand fit quite nicely with partner's hand. Bid a happy four spades.

B. ♠ K1076	You		Partner	
♥ A94	Pass	Pass	1♦	Pass
♦ 42	1♠	Pass	1NT	Pass
♣ J876				

112

This hand is about average. You have neither a fit nor a misfit, and your side has about half the deck. Pass and expect to take from six to eight tricks.

C. ♠ K1076	You		Partner	
♥ A94	—	1♠	Pass	1NT
♦ 42	Pass	Pass	2♦	Pass
♣ J876				

Your hand is going to be a bit disappointing to partner. You have less in high cards than he hopes to find and what you do have is not going to be too useful. You have not been doubled yet, but it will not come as a surprise if someone does object to two diamonds. You would far prefer to have the jack of diamonds instead of the king of spades.

A. ♠ AJ872	You		Partner	
♥ K54	1♠	Pass	2♥	Pass
♦ Q3	3♥	Pass	4♣	
♣ K53				

You should feel quite happy about this hand now. Partner is making a slam try and you have three prime cards for him. You should sign off in four hearts and hope partner can make one more try.

B. ♠ AJ872	You		Partner	
♥ K54	1♠	Pass	1NT	
♦ Q3				
♣ K53				

This is a normal one spade opening bid with nothing unusual about either strength or distribution. Pass.

C. ♠ AJ872	You		Partner	
♥ K54	1♠	2♥	Pass	Pass
♦ Q3				
♣ K53				

Nothing good here. Partner could not bid and, except for your ace, your cards are likely to be poorly placed.

A. ♠ J2	You		Partner	
♥ KQ107	—	—	1NT	Pass
♦ KJ942				
♣ J3				

You have a probable game. It is only a matter of determining the best one.

B. ♠ J2	You		Partner	
♥ KQ107	—	—	Pass	1NT
♦ KJ942	Pass	Pass	Pass	
♣ J3				

You have a slightly better than even chance of defeating one notrump.

C. ♠ J2	You		Partner	
♥ KQ107	—	—	3♥	3♠
♦ KJ942				
♣ J3				

The opponents can probably make four spades and conceivably have a slam. Your length in hearts greatly hurts your defensive chances.

A. ♠ 976542	You		Partner	
♥ K76	—	—	1♦	1♥
♦ A2	1♠	Pass	3♠	Pass
♣ 108				

Bid game and make it easily.

B. ♠ 976542	You		Partner	
♥ K76	Pass	Pass	1♦	Pass
♦ A2	1♠	Pass	1NT	
♣ 108				

Bid two spades. It will be a reasonable partscore.

C. ♠ 976542	You		Partner	
♥ K76	Pass	Pass	1♦	Dbl
♦ A2	1♠	3♥	Pass	4♥
♣ 108				

Not only has your heart king lessened in value, although it may well take a trick, but your partner is likely to lead a spade, which you do not want at all.

A. ♠ Q54	You		Partner	
♥ 92	—	—	1♠	2♣
♦ J873	Pass	Pass	3♦	
♣ 10642				

Not only does partner have a good hand, but it includes the two suits you can help. Almost always, a fit will be the only thing to make a bad hand turn into a good one. Jump to four spades.

B. ♠ Q54	You		Partner	
♥ 92	Pass	Pass	1♠	Pass
♦ J873	Pass	Pass		
♣ 10642				

This hand is actually a little better than average for this auction.

C. ♠ Q54	You		Partner	
♥ 92	—	3♠	Dbl	Pass
♦ J873				
♣ 10642				

Well? Pass, three notrump, four clubs or four diamonds are all available, and are all perfectly revolting. Who knows what is right?

A. ♠ KJ876	You		Partner	
♥ A42	—	3♥	Dbl	4♥
♦ K107				
♣ AQ				

This is not a bad hand in the first place, and it has gotten better fast. Partner has spade support, shown by his takeout double, and he cannot have more than one heart, assuming the opponents, bidding is reasonably sane. Try Blackwood and bid at least six spades.

B. ♠ KJ876	You		Partner	
♥ A42	1♠	Pass	1NT	Pass
♦ K107				
♣ AQ				

A raise to two notrump is OK, but no promises come with it. Game may or may not make.

C. ♠ KJ876	You		Partner	
♥ A42	—	1♠	Pass	2♥
♦ K107	Pass	3♥	Pass	4♥
♣ AQ				

Do you find this auction a bit surprising? You have a fat seventeen and the opponents have bid a game. It is just like you are not at the table. What do you think your chances are of beating four hearts? Should you double and expect to get rich or should you pass and hope they go down?

I hope you chose the latter course of action. Pass. Here is the reason. When opponents bid a game voluntarily, they will usually not go down very many unless they run into a bad trump break or a foul distribution of the side suits. In this hand you can see that trumps are breaking normally. Admittedly, you have the spade suit well stopped, but that will not be enough. Your minor suit honors will take some tricks, but your most likely result will be to hold them to contract. If you double, they may go down, but not more than one trick. Against that, they may redouble and make it, or worse, they may make it because your double told declarer how to play it.

A. ♠ K1086	You		Partner	
♥ AJ84	Pass	1♦	Pass	1♠
♦ 2	Pass	2♣	Pass	2♥
♣ 10983	Pass	2NT	Pass	3♥
	Pass	3NT	Pass	Pass

This time your hand has improved a bunch. The opponents have bid a game somewhat less than confidently. Their values are limited and at best they will make three notrump with an overtrick. That is what they think. But you know better. You have a stack in both suits bid on your right, and it is not unreasonable to expect partner to hold something similar in diamonds. This is a very good speculative double.

B. ♠ K1086	You		Partner	
♥ AJ84	—	Pass	1♦	Pass
♦ 2	1♥	Pass	2♥	Pass
♣ 10983				

This is a nice hand for two hearts. Pass and expect to make it.

C. ♠ K1086	You		Partner	
♥ AJ84	—	—	Pass	1♦
♦ 2	Pass	1♠	Pass	2♣
♣ 10983	Pass	3♥	Pass	3NT

The opponents are in three notrump again, but you should not dream of doubling. Firstly, your high cards are no longer favorably placed as in the earlier auction. And secondly, the opponents' strength has not been limited. Look closely at the auction. Either opponent may hold some extra values which would warrant a fast redouble.

A. ♠ AQ10	You		Partner	
♥ Q42	1♦	3♥	3♠	4♥
♦ KQ873				
♣ KQ				

The fact of so much heart bidding by the opponents suggests a singleton in partner's hand. If he has two aces, bid a slam.

B. ♠ AQ10	You		Partner	
♥ Q42	—	Pass	Pass	1♣
♦ KQ873	Dbl	Pass	1♥	Pass
♣ KQ	1NT			

You should not feel you have much in reserve for this sequence.

C. ♠ AQ10	You		Partner	
♥ Q42	—	1♠	Pass	2♥
♦ KQ873				
♣ KQ				

Do not bid! Pass! The opponents are marked for all of the outstanding high cards, leaving your partner with a nice zero. How will your hand play in say, three diamonds doubled, opposite a yarborough? Not pretty, is it?

In this section on evaluation, a large number of influences were considered which might affect your judgment. But it is an endless topic. Every hand brings forth new considerations.

If you had trouble with these hands, try them again. Each one has an endless number of auctions available which will suit the criteria for an answer. Or, if you wish, deal out some hands of your own and practice with them.

When you begin to find yourself loving certain cards and feeling warmly to others, or when you experience the dizzy sinking feeling when a nice twenty pointer skids into a bear market and slithers out at three or four, or less, then you can begin to feel confident of your judgment.

CHAPTER VIII   DEFENSE

When this book was originally in the planning stages, it had been my intention to look into the common errors of both play and defense as well as bidding. On reconsideration, however, the play section has been dropped and the defense section extended. The reason is simple enough. In the area of dummy play, the mistakes made are not sufficiently common so that any one topic stands out for special attention. This does not in any way mean that people have reached an adequate level of expertise in playing the dummy. It merely means that any given player will tend to play, or misplay, most hands at a certain level of efficiency.

I am sure this is because dummy play is more of an exact science than bidding and this in turn makes it easier to teach and learn. There are many excellent texts on play. Read them and learn them and you will do quite well. And, as you do so, you should note that the differences between one book and another are almost nonexistent. The styles of presentation may vary, the depth of analysis may differ, and one may cover areas omitted by another, but nowhere will you find two discussions on the same topic not agreeing on the basics.

Now look at bidding. There are systems, and styles, and individual tendencies. On one day one system may be better than another, this being determined by the success or failure of a finesse. Or perhaps you (or I, or anyone) felt more conservative today than yesterday, or was it foolhardy and reckless (if you went for eight hundred) or imaginative or innovative (if it made through a brilliant stroke in the play)? Whatever it is, the personal touch comes out in the bidding much more than in the play.

In the same way that bidding lends itself to the kinds of errors which can be identified and discussed, so too, do the errors of defense. This is because defense, like bidding, is a partnership game and the errors made are more often errors in *communication* rather than errors of execution.

If all of the above is confusing, skip it. Instead spend your time on the ensuing materials. Practical bridge is always more rewarding than theory.

Play to Third Hand at Notrump

This chapter will deal with one simple situation only. Your partner leads a small card against a notrump contract. Dummy plays a card you cannot beat. You have to decide what card to play from your holding in that suit.

Here are some card combinations for you to think about.

Partner leads this card	Dummy has these cards in the suit led and plays the italicized card	You have this holding in the suit led. What is your play?
5	Q*J*2	108
6	Q*J*2	1087
6	Q*J*2	10954
4	Q*J*2	53
7	Q*103*	94
6	Q*103*	972
6	Q*103*	9754
5	Q*103*	94
4	*Q*105	972
4	*Q*105	9763
3	*Q*105	J762
4	*Q*105	J82
5	*Q*7	J92
2	*Q*7	J8
5	*Q*7	1093
5	*Q*7	J108
5	*Q*7	J542
5	*Q*7	10942
5	*K*3	J97
6	*K*7	Q102
6	*K*4	QJ3

Well? What did you play? How strongly do you feel about it? When you choose a card, do you have a particular message in mind to tell your partner? Are you sure your partner understands that message? Honest?

Let's take a look at one of those situations.

Lead	Dummy	You
5	Q*J*2	1093

Which card is right, the three, nine, or ten? There is now in vogue a method of discarding which is called the Foster Echo. According to this rule, you should play your second highest card when you cannot beat the card played from dummy. Here then, you would be expected to play the nine. This has the effect of telling partner you have one higher card, in this case, the ten. Sometimes this piece of information is most useful. And sometimes it is not.

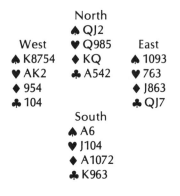

North
♠ QJ2
♥ Q985
♦ KQ
♣ A542

West
♠ K8754
♥ AK2
♦ 954
♣ 104

East
♠ 1093
♥ 763
♦ J863
♣ QJ7

South
♠ A6
♥ J104
♦ A1072
♣ K963

North	East	South	West
1♣	Pass	1♦	Pass
1♥	Pass	2NT	Pass
3NT	Pass	Pass	Pass

West led the spade five, won in dummy with the jack, on which East played the nine. West took the heart lead and cogitated. He knew East had the ten of spades, but that information was not much use at this moment. What West needed to know was how *many* spades did East have? If East began with three spades, declarer began with two. In this case, West might continue with a low spade, dropping declarer's now singleton ace. This defense, as you can see, sets three notrump. At the table, West guessed wrong and shifted to a diamond. The defense rested.

How can West tell, or is it impossible to solve this problem? The answer is really quite simple. If East plays the three, giving count, West will know how to continue the defense and three notrump will be down one.

Does this mean that giving count* is the answer? Not quite. In the following setup, East-West have a different problem to solve.

*Giving count means playing a high card to show an even number of cards, and a low card to show an odd number. You would play the underlined cards from the following combinations if you wished to give count.

10̲7   108̲42   109̲82   5̲432   109̲2   108̲6̲   109̲8̲
87532̲

120

```
                    North
                    ♠ Q2
                    ♥ Q985
                    ♦ KQ2
         West       ♣ A542      East
         ♠ K10754               ♠ J83
         ♥ AK2                  ♥ 763
         ♦ 954                  ♦ J863
         ♣ 108      South       ♣ QJ7
                    ♠ A96
                    ♥ J104
                    ♦ A107
                    ♣ K963
```

North	East	South	West
1♣	Pass	2NT	Pass
3NT	Pass	Pass	Pass

West again starts with the spade five and the spade queen in dummy wins. When West gets in with a heart, he has to guess again whether or not it is safe to lead another spade.

How would you have East-West solve this, short of making a good guess? Should East play the three, which under one rule shows an odd number of spades, or should East play the eight, which under the other rule shows one higher spade, which could be the nine? Neither rule works here, both of them leaving West with an out and out guess. Which is a bit silly. Somehow, choosing from two alternatives, neither of which works, seems a bit distressing. There must be something better. And there is.

Look once again at these two situations.

```
         Leader      Dummy
         K8754       QJ2
         K8754       Q2
```

In the first case, what does West want to know? In the second case, what does West want to know? What is the difference?

Here it is, in a nutshell. In the first case, West wants to know how many spades East has and in the second case, West wants to know if East has a high card in the suit. Is there any way for East-West to untangle the problem so as to answer both questions? Yes, there is a way, and considering the importance of the problem, the answer is delightfully simple.

When the dummy's holding in the suit led precludes East's having an honor in the suit, East gives a distributional count. When it *is* possible for East to have a critical card in the suit led, his signals should indicate that he does or does not have the card. Let's see these principles in action.

5   Q J 2   1073   When dummy plays the jack, you should
                                       play the three. This tells partner
you have an odd number of cards, either one, three or five. He will probably
be able to work out which it is. Partner will recognize that you cannot have
an honor in the suit because you would have played it.

7   Q J 3   10654   This time you play the six. Partner
                                        will probably be able to read this
card as a relatively high one. He will understand your play to mean you have
two or four cards in the suit and will proceed as he deems best.

6   Q J 2   103   Play the ten. Note that in this
                                      situation, your play does *not* show
you like the suit. It merely says you have an even number of cards in it, in this
case two cards.

    **RULE: When you give count, it must be clear to both you and partner that
you cannot hold an important card in the suit. This can only be the case
when dummy has two honors in the suit.**

6   Q J 3   1092
6   Q 10 7   93
6   K Q 3   10842
6   K J 3   83

When you are giving count signals, you should try to make it as easy as
possible on your partner. But when you are giving an even number signal,
you have to choose sometimes from an assortment of cards.

6   Q J 10   7432   Here, you can choose from the seven,
                                        four, or three. Anyone of which
theoretically gives count. Choose the seven. It is the loudest card you can
afford.
    "The loudest card you can afford." This phrase applies to all forms of
signals. When you want partner to get a message, be it count, as here, or an
encouraging card in some other situation, if you can afford a high card, play
it. The louder the card you can play, the more likely partner will notice it and
be able to understand it.

6   Q J 2   10942   Try not to signal with a ten spot,
                                        when you are showing four cards. It
is best to reserve it to show a doubleton. This is one of the few exceptions to
the "highest card you can afford" rule.

On the other side of the coin are those situations where your objective is to show partner if you do or do not have a crucial honor in the suit led. In all cases, the crucial honor will be the one just lower than the one played from dummy.

The Lead	The Dummy	Your Hand	
4	Q7	10852	You play the two, which tells partner you do not have the jack.

4	Q8	J73	The seven is the best you can do. It is the loudest card you can afford.

Partner wants to know if you have the jack. Tell him you do have it.

4	Q7	J103	You can afford the jack here because you have the ten to back it up.

4	Q7	1093	From the preceding situation you saw you would play the jack if you had the

J10 combination. The play of the ten guarantees the nine.

4	Q7	J92	Now the nine shows the jack.

This is the reason for what may seem like an unusual bit of discarding.

J102	J92	1092

These are the important holdings that partner will most want to know about and discarding as shown lets partner know exactly what you have with no ambiguity.

4	K7	Q52	When dummy plays the king, as opposed to the queen in the earlier examples,

the crucial card becomes the queen. Your discards should show possession or lack of possession of that card.

Unfortunately, the five is the loudest card you can afford.

4	K3	J82	When dummy plays the king, you in your discarding should ignore the

jack. Concern yourself with the queen only. It is the card immediately lower in rank to the one played from dummy.

The Lead	The Dummy	Your Hand	
4	K̲7	J972	Still the two.

| 4 | K̲3 | Q93 | You can encourage now. Play the nine. |

| 4 | K̲3 | QJ3 | The loudest card you can afford, the queen. You are not going to play the |

three. That would be quite uninformative, nor do you play the jack, as that
would convey misinformation.

| 4 | K̲3 | J̲107 | The jack here denies the queen. With both the queen and jack, you would |

play the queen. Therefore the jack denies the queen, and shows the ten.

| 4 | K̲3 | Q1̲07 | The ten here shows the queen. Again play the loudest card you can afford. |
| | QJ3 | Q1̲03 | J̲103 |

This allows you to show exactly what you have in the three most important
situations.

Some care must be taken not to confuse the two situations. When dummy
has only one high card, your problem is easy. If dummy plays the king, you
signal whether you do or do not have the queen. Likewise, when dummy
plays the queen, you signal possession or non-possession of the jack.

When dummy has two honor cards, and plays one, there may be a
problem as in the following two cases.

The Lead	The Dummy		
4	K̲J3		Here, it is possible for East to have the queen, so he should signal

to West whether he does or does not hold that card.

| 4 | KJ̲3 | | This time, if East has the queen, he will play it. When he does not have |

the queen to play, East signals distribution.

| 4 | Q̲102 | | Like the preceding situation, East can have the jack, so he should signal if he does. |

| 4 | Q1̲02 | | Again, East would play the jack if he had it, so if he does not have the jack, he signals distribution. |

4	KQ2	
4	QJ2	When dummy's two honors are touching,
4	QJ10	as in the examples on the left, there
4	KQJ	cannot be any problem about the

possession of lesser honor cards because they are in plain sight in the dummy. Count should always be given and never misunderstood.

If you do decide to switch from whatever you are using to these signals, you will find they present almost no problems at all. If a problem does come up and you get a bad result, ask yourself if your previous system of discards would have solved it.

The following hand is presented in anticipation of your suffering from a similar disaster in the forseeable future.

```
                        North
                        ♠ Q8
                        ♥ KJ4
                        ♦ 1092
          West          ♣ AQJ109    East
          ♠ AJ963                   ♠ 10542
          ♥ 1093                    ♥ 7652
          ♦ K4                      ♦ 765
          ♣ 532         South       ♣ K8
                        ♠ K7
                        ♥ AQ8
                        ♦ AQJ83
                        ♣ 764
```

North	East	South	West
1♣	Pass	1♦	Pass
2♣	Pass	3NT	All Pass

West's spade lead went to dummy's queen. East played the two, correctly implying he did not hold the jack. Declarer now took a diamond finesse, losing to West's king.

Well, it is clear from here that if West bangs down the spade ace, three notrump will be beaten. But not at all unreasonably, West shifted to a heart and declarer grabbed his nine tricks.

How could West tell? Perhaps, looking at the dummy, West should guess to try the spade ace, but there is really no way to know for sure, if you are signaling as I have recommended.

The solution? There isn't one. There is no perfect system of signals, short of hand signals. The best you can do is to find the one which most consistently gets good results. If you had been playing the Foster Echo here, you would have had the same bad result. Only if you signaled distribution all the time could you avoid this debacle.

Should you signal distribution all the time? I think not. You can construct your own hands to show why that system would be a loser if used with no discretion.

Other than the above hand though, there should not be much trouble for you with these signals. They are fairly simple, reasonably comprehensive, and any pair can arrive at an understanding as to what their discards mean.

CHAPTER IX   SUIT PREFERENCE...THE ART OF CONFUSION

When bridge was in the early stages of development, defense was a fairly simple affair. If partner led a suit you liked, you encouraged with a high card. If partner led a suit you did not like, you played a small card. When the system worked, great. If not, unlucky. Then one day, after a typically poor result, a defender made the standard remark of "If you had shifted to a diamond, we could have set them." And the reply was "How could I tell?" Usually this conversation continued and ended with, "I don't know" and the matter was dropped.

But on this day the problem was pursued in a fit of understandable frustration. Well, it took a long time, but someone finally came up with a solution. It was called the suit preference signal.

In theory, it works this way.

```
                North
                ♠ AQ87
                ♥ KQ8
                ♦ J1098
West            ♣ QJ          East
♠ 32                          ♠ 9            North   East    South   West
♥ 4                           ♥ A106532       —       —      1♠     Pass
♦ 65432                       ♦ A7           3♠      Pass    4♠     All Pass
♣ 98764         South         ♣ K532
                ♠ KJ10654
                ♥ J97
                ♦ KQ
                ♣ A10
```

West leads the heart four to East's ace. East returns the ten for West to ruff. West must now guess correctly whether East has a re-entry in clubs or diamonds. Suit preference avoids the guess. West can tell from the size of the heart returned by East which suit East's entry is in. The ten of hearts is clearly an "unnecessarily high" card and suggests therefore the lead of the higher ranking suit of the suits in question. Properly used here, suit preference will set four spades, as West will lead a diamond at trick three thus getting a second heart ruff.

Or perhaps the suit preference will work like this.

```
              North
              ♠ KJ93
              ♥ 4
              ♦ K1097
West          ♣ K1097    East
♠ 2                      ♠ ———        North    East     South    West
♥ AQJ97653               ♥ K102
♦ 64                     ♦ AQJ532     —        —        1♠       4♥
♣ 64          South      ♣ 8532       4♠       5♥       6♠       All Pass
              ♠ AQ1087654
              ♥ 8
              ♦ 8
              ♣ AQJ
```

This auction is typical of the guessing games that are played when everyone has a good hand and both sides have a fit. South's leap to six spades is not unreasonable. Who knows what anyone can make? As it is, only accurate defense can defeat the contract. West cashes the heart ace and must immediately lead a diamond or it is all over for the defense. How does East get West to lead a diamond? He does it by playing an "unnecessarily high" heart on the first trick. Here that card should be the king, in keeping with the "loudest card you can afford" rule for defenders.

While the ten might get the message across, the play of the king will surely shock the sensibilities of the most lethargic of defenders. The result is one down when West finds the diamond shift. All very nice.

In practice, however, suit preferences seem to lead to results like these.

```
              North
              ♠ Q54
              ♥ 8543
              ♦ Q76
West          ♣ KQJ      East
♠ A9863                  ♠ J102       North    East     South    West
♥ J7                     ♥ 9          —        —        —        Pass
♦ A82                    ♦ KJ103
♣ 764        South       ♣ 109852     Pass     Pass     1♥       1♠
             ♠ K7                     2♥       2♠       4♥       All Pass
             ♥ AKQ1062
             ♦ 954
             ♣ A3
```

West led the ace of spades and East played the deuce. For some reason West decided that was a suit preference signal calling for a club lead. Declarer did not mind the club shift at all. An overtrick was made on a hand which should go down.

Next case.

```
                North
                ♠ A76
                ♥ Q965
                ♦ 864
West            ♣ KQ10    East
♠ 9853                    ♠ Q1042    North    East     South    West
♥ 103                     ♥ J87      —        Pass     1NT      Pass
♦ AK10                    ♦ QJ52     2♣       Pass     2♥       Pass
♣ 6543          South     ♣ 87       4♥       All Pass
                ♠ KJ
                ♥ AK42
                ♦ 973
                ♣ AJ92
```

West led the king of diamonds, and East played the queen. This is a standard signal which is intended to show the jack. The opening leader can continue as he sees best. If he wishes, he can underlead his ace to partner's known jack should he wish. In the actual hand, four hearts can be defeated if the defense cashes three diamonds and East then leads the thirteenth diamond for an "uppercut." The defense will come to a trump trick no matter how declarer twists and turns.

What actually happened was that West decided to treat the diamond queen as a suit preference and switched smartly to a spade. This did not work at all. The result was no longer down one. Instead an overtrick was made by declarer.

```
                North
                ♠ A92
                ♥ K54
                ♦ 92
West            ♣ KQJ54   East
♠ QJ84                    ♠ K105     North    East     South    West
♥ Q1092                   ♥ 8763     —        Pass     1NT      Pass
♦ K3                      ♦ 854      3NT      All Pass
♣ 863           South     ♣ 1097
                ♠ 763
                ♥ AJ
                ♦ AQJ1076
                ♣ A2
```

This one will be hard to believe. You may not like the auction either, but it happened. Anyway, if it had gone otherwise, there might have been no story. West led the spade four, and declarer, visualizing thirteen tricks if the

129

diamond finesse worked, grabbed the ace. East correctly volunteered the ten of spades. Declarer eventually tried the diamond finesse, losing of course. West took the diamond king and led . . . the queen of hearts! A speechless East could only marvel as declarer fanned the rest of the hand.

What happened, of course, was that West had interpreted the ten of spades as a suit preference signal. This was a bit hard on East who had meant nothing of the sort.

No, this hand did not come out of Ripley's "Believe It Or Not." But it might as well have.

Perhaps all of this is causing you to give up the idea of using suit preference signals, or even abandoning them if you use them already. That was not my intention. Don't. Most definitely do not give them up. Properly used, suit preference signals are a wonderful weapon which can bring sorely needed relief to harrassed defenders.

Just remember that these signals are an aid in defense and are in no way intended to be the mainstay. If you will follow this one rule, you will have no problems with suit preferences.

RULE: Never interpret partner's card as a suit preference if it can logically mean anything else.

This means that suit preference is the *last* meaning you assign to partner's cards. (There are some exceptions, but they are standard. These are discussed shortly.)

Here are some typically mishandled situations. The first one is a classic. It happens again and again and again.

West, holding the ace and king of some suit, leads the king, and East plays the queen. East has either the jack as well or the queen was a singleton. West will rarely have any difficulty telling which it is and should have no trouble knowing what to do. Perhaps one percent of the time, the play of the queen will be properly intended as a suit preference signal.

This means that if West leads the king and East plays the queen, it should be interpreted as a suit preference one time in a hundred. Unfortunately, it is so interpreted about twenty times in a hundred. West sees the queen and hastens to make a disastrous shift. This is expensive and sad. So much is lost at the expense of one of the best and simplest of defensive signals.

A less common situation is East playing a high card which is intended to be either encouraging or informative. For instance:

$$J54$$
$$AK982 \qquad Q103$$
$$76$$

West leads the king against three notrump. East encourages with the ten. How else can East say he likes the suit? This should lead to five fast tricks for the defense *all* the time. But for some reason, something bad happens every now and then. West decides to shift. Declarer then scores up three notrump, instead of one down.

Notice that the rule would easily defeat three notrump. East's card *can* be interpreted as encouraging, so it *should* be.

3

AK842   J1097

Q65

Here, West again leads the king against three notrump. East correctly plays the jack. This tells West that East likes the suit and at the same time it denies the queen. West is expected to work out the best defense in light of this fact. It may be right to continue the suit or it may be right to shift to another suit. However, if West does decide to shift suits, he does so on the merits of the hand alone. There is no suit preference whatsoever in East's play of the jack, and West must be aware of this fact.

If defenders do not have enough problems with high cards, look what happens when they start to play small ones.

North
♠ 1076
♥ KJ75
♦ KJ108
♣ J2

West		East				
♠ QJ983		♠ K2	North	East	South	West
♦ 642		♥ 98	—	—	1NT	Pass
♦ A93		♦ 6542	2♣	Pass	2♥	Pass
♣ Q4	South	♣ K10963	4♥	All Pass		
	♠ A54					
	♥ AQ103					
	♦ Q7					
	♣ A875					

North bid two clubs, asking for a major suit, and South obliged with two hearts. North proceeded to game.

West led the spade queen. East could not play the king as that would allow the ten in dummy to become a trick. So East played the two. Now if declarer had taken this trick, as he should have, four hearts would be unbeatable. On winning the ace of diamonds, the defense would be unable to untangle the spade suit and declarer would have time to discard his spade loser. (South must concede the diamond before drawing the third round of trump.)

In any case, declarer erred and played low to trick one. This gave the defense the chance to overcome the blockage in spades. So what happened? Did West lead a spade to East's king? Did declarer pay for his error? No indeed. West, alertly observing East's two of spades, shifted with a learned air to the club queen. Having goofed by not capturing the queen of spades, declarer did not repeat his mistake by ducking the club queen as well. Four

131

hearts making was the end result of this hand.
Why?

It seems that West thought East's two of spades called for a club shift. This was of course not the case. Not only did East not want a club shift, he did not want any shift at all. Had West given any thought to the spade suit, he would have worked out what was happening and would have continued the suit. Unfortunately he did not do either.

Usually, the situation is not as complex as the one just discussed. A more common situation is something like the next case.

```
              North
              ♠ 10653
              ♥ KQ7
              ♦ KQ
West          ♣ QJ98        East
♠ AKJ                       ♠ 842
♥ 103                       ♥ 652
♦ J654                      ♦ A9832
♣ 10763       South         ♣ 42
              ♠ Q97
              ♥ AJ984
              ♦ 107
              ♣ AK5
```

The bidding was direct and simple. One heart by South, three hearts by North, and South continued to game. West led the king of spades and East played the two. What does that two of spades mean? If you apply the rule of this chapter to determine what partner's card means, you will find that:

1. The spade two *can* be a discouraging card;

2. Therefore it *is* a discouraging card. It says, "I don't like spades." Nothing else at all is implied.

When partner tells you not to lead a suit, by playing a small card, he is expecting you to work out the best continuation. It may be that you should continue the suit in spite of partner's opinion. Or it may be right to shift. All you know is that partner does not like your suit. Remember that partner cannot tell you that he does not like your suit and at the same time tell you what he does like. Do not forget this. One card cannot be played and mean two things at the same time.

In the hand in question, West is faced with a common problem. To shift, and if so, to what? (Hand repeated for convenience.)

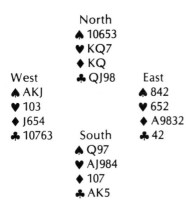

```
                North
                ♠ 10653
                ♥ KQ7
                ♦ KQ
West            ♣ QJ98          East
♠ AKJ                           ♠ 842
♥ 103                           ♥ 652
♦ J654                          ♦ A9832
♣ 10763         South           ♣ 42
                ♠ Q97
                ♥ AJ984
                ♦ 107
                ♣ AK5
```

West can see that continuing spades will probably set up declarer's queen. Some shift is therefore in order. If West decides to lead a club, declarer will have no problem. A diamond switch on the other hand will lead to one down.

A thinking defender will lead the diamond on the theory that declarer will not be able, if he has the diamond ace, to discard any losers. On the other hand, if declarer has the ace and king of clubs, he may be able to get rid of his spade losers. The thinking defender realizes that if East has the ace of clubs, it will wait. So West leads a diamond expecting that if four hearts can be set, this will do it, eventually.

A careless defender will lead a club, oblivious to the above, or perhaps under the impression that the spade two called for a club shift. Whatever the reason, be it from laziness or a misunderstanding as to the true meaning of the spade two, the club shift will not work.

So far, this entire chapter has been discussing what is not a suit preference signal. Once you understand what is not a suit preference signal, it will be easy to appreciate what is.

Suit preference can be divided into two areas. (1) Standard situations which demand suit preference. (2) Unusual cards played during the defense of a hand which cannot have a normal meaning. These cards will generally be spectacular in that one would not expect to see them played.

Standard Situations

The common defensive situations where suit preference signals are almost mandatory include the following two. (1) Telling partner where your entry is, if any, to run a suit against a notrump contract. (2) Telling partner where your entry is, if any, to give him a ruff.

Here are some example hands.

```
              North
              ♠ 8764
              ♥ QJ32
              ♦ 762
West          ♣ K3        East
♠ 3                       ♠ AJ1092      North    East      South    West
♥ 54                      ♥ A6          Pass     1♠        2♥       Pass
♦ J109854                 ♦ AQ          Pass     3♣        Pass     Pass
♣ J654        South       ♣ Q1098       3♥       All Pass
              ♠ KQ5
              ♥ K10987
              ♦ K3
              ♣ A72
```

West leads his singleton spade to East's ace. East's return of the spade jack is covered by South and ruffed by West. Now if West returns a club, on the theory that East bid them, declarer will make three hearts. South will lead a trump and West will no longer be able to trump another spade.

West, if he is reasonably wide awake, will note that East returned the jack of spades, as opposed to one of his smaller ones. This should alert West to the fact that East wishes a diamond return as opposed to a club return, the auction not withstanding.

This is the rule to follow when you are leading a suit for partner to ruff. The lead of a high card requests partner to return the higher ranking of the remaining two suits. Conversely, the lead of a low card asks for the return of the lower of the two suits.

```
                 North
                 ♠ J83
                 ♥ Q
                 ♦ Q10843
West        ♣ KJ94   East            North   East   South   West
♠ 97                 ♠ 65            —       —      —       3♥
♥ KJ109765           ♥ 8432          Pass    4♥     4♠      All Pass
♦ 2                  ♦ A965
♣ Q63       South    ♣ A105
                 ♠ AKQ1042
                 ♥ A
                 ♦ KJ7
                 ♣ 852
```

West leads his diamond. East takes the ace and returns the five which West trumps. Again, West must pay attention to the card East returned. It was in fact the five. A quick look at the diamonds in view, the three and four in dummy, and the two, which was led, shows that the five is East's lowest diamond. This should cause West to reconsider, if he was reaching for a heart, and to lead instead a club. It certainly does not look appealing to lead a club, with the king jack sitting in the dummy, but as you can see, nothing else will do.

Sometimes the spot cards are deceiving. You may be caught off-guard by the fact that a card looked "big" or "small."

```
                 North
                 ♠ KQ9
                 ♥ A5
                 ♦ A7
West        ♣ 876432  East           North   East   South   West
♠ 32                  ♠ A4           1♣      Pass   1♠      Pass
♥ Q932                ♥ 108764        2♠      Pass   4♠      All Pass
♦ J95432              ♦ K86
♣ 5         South     ♣ A109
                 ♠ J108765
                 ♥ KJ
                 ♦ Q10
                 ♣ KQJ
```

West, once again, gets off to the lead of his singleton. East obligingly takes the trick and considers. East can see that if West, after trumping the club, can be induced to lead a diamond, South will probably go down. So East returns the club nine, which West duly trumps.

Question: Is a nine spot a big card or a little card?

In this case, it is the littlest one East has, so by definition, it is little and therefore requests a diamond return. This means that West must be very careful to analyze each suit preference card in light of the situation in hand.

The problem of big and small cards works both ways.

```
              North
              ♠ J109875
              ♥ 5
              ♦ QJ4
West          ♣ QJ5         East          North   East   South   West
♠ 6                         ♠ A432         —       —      —       Pass
♥ J973                      ♥ 2            Pass    1♣     4♥      All Pass
♦ 1073                      ♦ A962
♣ 76432       South         ♣ K1098
              ♠ KQ
              ♥ AKQ10864
              ♦ K85
              ♣ A
```

South decided to give up on a slam when East opened the bidding and went quickly to four hearts.

West, holding five clubs, felt there would be no future in leading them. He opened therefore his singleton spade. East won the ace and returned the four for West to trump. A diamond return will defeat four hearts as East will continue with another spade. West's heart jack will be promoted into the setting trick. Should West know that a diamond is the right lead or can he tell? He should know. A quick glance at the spade suit shows that only the three and the two are missing. The four is actually the highest spade available for East to return. As you can see, suit preferences are not for the lazy defenders.

Now and then, you will find yourself giving partner a ruff and you really do not care what he returns because you have no possible entry. Strangely, when this is the case, you have to be more careful than ever in your choice of card to lead.

Here is what happens when the defense gets careless.

	North					
	♠ QJ73					
	♥ Q95					
	♦ KQ10					

West		East	North	East	South	West
♠ 54	♣ K54	♠ A82	—	—	1NT	Pass
♥ 2		♥ A108763	2♣	Pass	2♠	Pass
♦ 97653		♦ 82	4♠	All Pass		
♣ Q8763	South	♣ J2				
	♠ K1096					
	♥ KJ4					
	♦ AJ4					
	♣ A109					

West starts his singleton heart which East takes. East can see one heart ruff and the trump ace. The setting trick, if any, will have to come from clubs. (West will not be able to trump another heart as he will be out of trump by the time East gets in again.) East therefore returns the heart ten. In this case, East is not really trying to get a diamond return but rather trying to keep West from making a damaging club return. Look what happens if West returns a club. (From West's point of view, East could have the club or diamond ace instead of the spade ace, in which case, leading over to that ace will secure a second heart ruff.) On a club return, East must play the jack to force out declarer's ace. Subsequently, South can lead the club ten in order to finesse against West's queen.

But if West returns a diamond, declarer will not be able to avoid losing a club trick. East's return of the heart ten is not looking for something good. Rather it is looking to avoid something bad.

Here is another example.

	North					
	♠ Q64					
	♥ 1054					
	♦ Q7543					

West		East	North	East	South	West
♠ AJ1087	♣ A106	♠ 9532	—	—	—	Pass
♥ 632		♥ KQ	Pass	Pass	1♥	1♠
♦ 8		♦ A962	2♥	2♠	3♥	Pass
♣ K975	South	♣ 83	4♥	All Pass		
	♠ K					
	♥ AJ987					
	♦ KJ10					
	♣ QJ42					

If you do not care for the four heart bid, well neither do I. But look what happens if the defense gets careless or if the defenders do not trust each other.

West leads a diamond and gets his ruff at trick two. What should he continue with at the third trick? If West returns a low spade as a result of East's spade raise, the defense will do quite poorly. If, however, West pays attention to East's diamond spot, and if he trusts East to know what he is doing, then West will assume East does not have the spade king.

Are you wondering which diamond East returned? Good. It was the two. East could see the king and queen of hearts in his own hand and knew they would represent the defense's third trick, after getting a diamond ruff. East also knew that West would hardly expect East to have high cards in hearts and would probably assume East's high cards were elsewhere. East realized that West would expect East to have a spade honor for the raise to two spades. Therefore the diamond selected by East at trick two was an effort to tell West not to underlead in spades.

West may decide to lead a club, hoping for the queen in East's hand. Or West may cash the spade ace. Or West may just exit with a trump. The one thing a trusting West will not do is lead a low spade.

There are also occasions where a defender can lead a card which is clearly a "non-preference" signal saying "I do not care what you lead next." This happens when the hand leading the "suit preference" card is known to have quite a few cards in the suit led. If the card selected is a middle card as opposed to a high or low one, the meaning is one of neutrality. It tells partner to use his own judgment. A hand that has overcalled or pre-empted is known to have at least five or more of a suit. It would be easy in this case to give a "non-preference." This might be the situation:

```
              North
              ♠ 1087
              ♥ KJ9
              ♦ 10764
West          ♣ A102    East
♠ 3                     ♠ AQJ9652
♥ 43                    ♥ 52
♦ KQ98                  ♦ 52
♣ K97654    South       ♣ J3
              ♠ K4
              ♥ AQ10876
              ♦ AJ3
              ♣ Q8
```

North	East	South	West
Pass	3♠	4♥	All Pass

The spade three goes to East's ace. East knows he can give his partner a ruff and does so. The card selected is the spade six (or nine). West should realize that either of these cards cannot be asking for a specific shift. After ruffing in at trick two, West will see the dangers of leading clubs or diamonds and will get out with a trump. Declarer can still make four hearts, but this defense will make it harder for him. If, instead, West leads clubs or diamonds, declarer will have a relatively easy time making his contract.

Another way the "non-preference" aspect of a card can become clear is the following situation.

KQJ103

2   A98754

6

West leads the two to East's ace. If East has no preferences, he can return the seven. When declarer shows out, West will know exactly East's holding and the meaning of the seven should be clear.

It often happens that a defender leads a singleton and his partner cannot win the first trick. However, there is the chance that the opening leader can get in again, in time to get a ruff. It only remains for the opening leader to guess what suit to lead to get his partner in with to get that ruff. The answer can sometimes be found in the card partner played at trick one. Was it a big one? Was it a low one? Or, and most important of all, if it could have been an encouraging or discouraging card, it is not a suit preference signal at all.

Remember. If your partner cannot tell that you are leading a singleton, he will be trying to tell you whether or not he wants you to continue the suit. His play therefore will be "encourage-discourage" rather than suit preference.

But, if your card is an obvious singleton, his card will be suit preference and you should so interpret it.

	North		North	East	South	West
	♠ AKQ107					
	♥ Q102					
	♦ K102					
West	♣ 53	East	1♠	Pass	2♥	Pass
♠ 2		♠ J9864	3♥	Pass	4♥	All Pass
♥ A65		♥ 7				
♦ 97643		♦ AQ5				
♣ J982	South	♣ Q1076				
	♠ 53					
	♥ KJ9843					
	♦ J8					
	♣ AK4					

West's lead of the spade two is easily recognized as a singleton. East's correct play is the spade nine. West will know now to shift to a diamond rather than to a club.

```
              North
              ♠ J96
              ♥ 84
              ♦ AQ54
West          ♣ J1087     East          North     East     South    West
♠ K10832                  ♠ AQ54        —         Pass     1♣      Pass
♥ 97632                   ♥ KJ105       2♣        Dbl      5♣      Dbl
♦ 7                       ♦ 10862       All Pass
♣ A5          South       ♣ 3
              ♠ 7
              ♥ AQ
              ♦ KJ93
              ♣ KQ9642
```

West's diamond lead is taken by North's ace. East plays the two. West takes the club lead at trick two and must guess whether to lead a heart or a spade. If West guesses to lead a spade, five clubs will go down because East will be able to give West the diamond ruff. If West leads a heart, five clubs will make. What is the solution? There is none. There is no way for East to know that West has a singleton diamond. Therefore he is busy telling West that diamonds have no future for the defense.

West should realize this and his choice of what to lead at trick three must take this into consideration. If you learn the lesson of this hand, and understand that West has no reason to infer any suit preference connotations to the diamond two, you will be very well placed.

One last example in this family.

```
              North
              ♠ KQJ862
              ♥ Q
              ♦ Q54
West          ♣ Q32       East          North     East     South    West
♠ A                       ♠ 109753      1♠        Pass     2♦      Pass
♥ 5432                    ♥ A76         2♠        Pass     3♥      Pass
♦ J97                     ♦ 2           4♦        Pass     4NT     Pass
♣ 87654       South       ♣ KJ109       5♣        Pass     5♦      All Pass
              ♠ 4
              ♥ KJ1098
              ♦ AK10073
              ♣ A
```

West cashed the ace of spades, hoping to put East in with a club. East could see that West's lead was probably a singleton and played the spade ten. If West had two spades, declarer would ruff the spade lead and nothing anyone did would effect the outcome. But if West did have a stiff spade, it was imperative to get West to shift to a heart. That is what the ten of spades said. A heart shift leads to down one because the ensuing spade lead sets up a sure trick for West's J97 of diamonds.

Playing in a notrump contract lends itself to fewer standard suit preference situations than suit contracts. But they are no less important. The mandatory suit preferences at notrump are usually intended to show where an entry may be to run a good suit.

It might look like one of the following.

```
              North
              ♠ A65
              ♥ Q54
              ♦ A10987
West          ♣ J6      East        North   East      South   West
♠ KQJ102                ♠ 43        Pass    Pass      1NT     Pass
♥ A76                   ♥ 10982     3NT     All Pass
♦ 42                    ♦ K53
♣ 983         South     ♣ 7542
              ♠ 987
              ♥ KJ
              ♦ QJ6
              ♣ AKQ10
```

West leads the spade king which declarer ducks. Declarer ducks West's queen of spades as well. West continues a third round which declarer must win. West hopes East can get in soon enough to lead to West's heart ace and the good spades. By leading the spade jack rather than a careless two, West can tell East to lead a heart rather than a club.

Similarly.

```
              North
              ♠ J5
              ♥ KJ7
              ♦ Q1076
West          ♣ KJ73    East        North   East      South   West
♠ Q8762                 ♠ A94       —       —         1♦      Pass
♥ 106                   ♥ 9843      2♣      Pass      2♦      Pass
♦ 954                   ♦ A         3♦      Pass      3NT     All Pass
♣ A82         South     ♣ 109654
              ♠ K103
              ♥ AQ52
              ♦ KJ832
              ♣ Q
```

West leads the spade six to East's ace. The spade return is ducked to West's queen. As before, West wants to tell East what suit to return, should East get in. West's lead at trick three is the spade two, telling East to lead a club.

Signals in Non-Mandatory Situations

Usually after a hand has gotten underway, there will not be very many standard situations which demand suit preference signals. Rather, a number of situations come up where you find yourself thinking, "It would be nice if partner would lead a club." Or perhaps you would like partner to lead a spade. Whatever the case, you would like to be able to get partner to do something specific.

The way you make your wish come true, if possible, is to play a card which is abnormal in that one would hardly expect to see it played. As in the mandatory suit preference situations, the size of the card played determines its suit preference qualities. The difference is that partner will not be expecting a suit preference. Only an exceptional unusual, or "loud" card will make itself felt by your partner for what it is.

Bear in mind that whenever you play or see your partner play, an unusual card, the first thing the defense should think of is "Is it an *encouraging-discouraging signal* or is it giving *count*." Only if partner's card cannot possibly fall into one of these categories should it be treated as a suit preference signal.

Let's see some examples of this at work. The following are typical of the problems the opening leader may have at trick one.

	Auction		West & Lead	Your Hand & Dummy		Partner's Card	Declarer's Card
North	East	South					
—	—	—	3♠	♠ A1098632	♠ KJ	Q	4
				♥ 43	♥ KQ7		
3NT	4♠	6♣	Pass	♦ J10	♦ KQ743		
Pass	Pass			♣ J2	♣ AQ2		

Partner's card is clearly suit preference. It is an abnormally high card which is not usually associated with encouraging or discouraging signals.

	Auction		West & Lead	Your Hand & Dummy		Partner's Card	Declarer's Card
North	East	South					
—	1♠	2♥	2♠	♠ KQ4	♠ 1073	J	5
				♥ J3	♥ K97		
3♥	Pass	4♥	Pass	♦ 9876	♦ KJ54		
Pass	Pass			♣ 10972	♣ KJ5		

Partner's jack is an unnecessarily high card which commands a shift, in this case to diamonds.

	Auction		West & Lead	Your Hand & Dummy		Partner's Card	Declarer's Card
North	East	South					
—	—	—	1♠	♠ AK952	♠ 863	Q	7
				♥ 42	♥ J7		
Pass	2♠	3♥	Pass	♦ KJ7	♦ Q54		
Pass	Pass			♣ Q94	♣ J10832		

This is the standard play to show the queen and jack. Your partner is telling you that you can get into his hand if you wish.

	Auction			Your Hand & Lead	Dummy	Partner's Card	Declarer's Card
North	East	South	West	♠ AK862	♠ J73	Q	5
—	—	—	1♠	♥ 7	♥ Q104		
Pass	2♠	3♥	Pass	♦ 10982	♦ J754		
4♥	All Pass			♣ KJ10	♣ AQ4		

Unless you are in the habit of raising with a doubleton queen, East's play should be a request for a diamond switch. The normal meaning of showing the jack does not apply here as the jack is in the dummy.

North	East	South	West	♠ J3	♠ Q762	2	3
—	Pass	1♦	1♥	♥ AK862	♥ J9Z		
Pass	Pass	1♠	Pass	♦ AJ7	♦ Q3		
2♠	All Pass			♣ Q42	♣ J987		

Partner's play of the two here implies a dislike of hearts. It says nothing about what to shift to. A very common error for defenders to make in this situation is to shift to a club.

RULE. Except for the standard suit preference situation, it is almost impossible to get partner to shift to a club. You cannot combine the message "don't lead your suit" with "shift to clubs."

Let's go over to the other side of the table and see how third hand might vary its play in the interest of suit preference.

	Auction			Partner's Lead	Dummy	Your Hand
North	East	South	West	Heart K	♠ AJ876	♠ KQ103
—	—	—	1♥		♥ Q86	♥ J1053
1♠	2♥	3♣	All Pass		♦ KJ8	♦ 1076
					♣ Q2	♣ 98

If you play the jack, it should have the effect of getting partner to shift to a spade. You cannot have a doubleton heart or you would not raise partner to two hearts.

North	East	South	West	Spade K	♠ 832	♠ Q94
—	—	—	1♠		♥ Q94	♥ KJ107
Pass	2♠	3♣	All Pass		♦ Q862	♦ J1043
					♣ 1063	♣ 75

There is no card you can play which will get partner to shift to hearts. If you play the nine, it will be read as a normal come on. If you play the queen, it will be interpreted as showing the jack as well. It would be a bit embarrassing if your partner underled his spade ace to your supposed jack and declarer produced it instead of you.

	Auction			Partner's Lead	Dummy	Your Hand
North	East	South	West	Spade A	♠ Q	♠ KJ865
—	—	1♥	1♠		♥ K108765	♥ 42
4♥	4♠	5♥	Pass		♦ K10872	♦ ——
Pass	5♠	Pass	Pass		♣ 9	♣ J87632
6♥	Dbl	All Pass				

This one is easy. Assuming the spade ace is not ruffed, you can defeat six hearts by getting partner to switch to diamonds. This can be done in no uncertain terms by playing the king of spades.

Going a bit further, you can sometimes use suit preference to trick two when it was not possible at trick one. This happens when you are able to begin one message and can then change to another. It is easier to show than to describe.

```
                North
                ♠ 763
                ♥ Q82
                ♦ J73
West            ♣ AQ104        East        North   East    South   West
♠ AK1084                       ♠ Q95       —       —       —       1♠
♥ 954                          ♥ KJ106     Pass    2♠      3♦      All Pass
♦ A5                           ♦ 1042
♣ 875           South          ♣ 632
                ♠ J2
                ♥ A73
                ♦ KQ986
                ♣ KJ9
```

West leads the king of spades. From an earlier example you have already seen that you cannot get partner to shift to a heart. At least you cannot get him to shift to a heart at trick two. There is a way however to get him to switch at the third trick. You do this by starting with the nine. Partner will continue with the ace and you will now drop the queen of spades. Now the message will be clear to partner and a heart shift should ensue.

Notice that you cannot make this play if it can set up a trick for declarer. In this case it is safe (if you play five card majors) to drop the queen because there is no combination of spades which can cost you a trick. From the dummy, it is clear that no matter what declarer's two spades are, the seven in dummy cannot take a trick.

144

If dummy's spades were 1092 and yours were Q87, playing the eight and then the queen could lose a trick if declarer began with the doubleton jack. A similar example.

```
                North
                ♠ J7
                ♥ Q86
                ♦ Q872
West            ♣ Q752        East
♠ KQ864                       ♠ A1082
♥ J10                         ♥ 75
♦ A109                        ♦ 6543
♣ J84           South         ♣ K109
                ♠ 43
                ♥ AK9432
                ♦ KJ
                ♣ A63
```

North	East	South	West
—	—	—	Pass
Pass	Pass	1♥	Dbl
Pass	1♠	2♥	Pass
Pass	2♠	Pass	Pass
3♥	All Pass		

West leads the king of spades and East wishes to encourage a club switch. This cannot be done at trick one, but it may be accomplished by trick two. East can, for example, overtake the spade and return the two. This sequence of plays should be sufficiently unusual to alert West. West will not expect East to have a doubleton spade, as he bid them twice. A club shift is the only logical answer and if West switches to the jack, three hearts will go down.

Had East wanted a diamond switch, he would play either (1) the eight followed by the ten; or (2) the ace, and return the ten (or eight).

```
                North
                ♠ K1082
                ♥ QJ4
                ♦ AJ72
West            ♣ Q5          East
♠ J9                          ♠ 7654
♥ 763                         ♥ A2
♦ K6                          ♦ Q1094
♣ AKJ984        South         ♣ 1032
                ♠ AQ3
                ♥ K10985
                ♦ 853
                ♣ 76
```

North	East	South	West
1♦	Pass	1♥	2♣
Pass	Pass	2♥	Pass
Pass	3♣	Pass	Pass
3♥	All Pass		

West leads the king of clubs and East plays the two. On the ace of clubs, East plays the three. The things West knows for sure are that East has the club ten (he raised to three clubs) and that East did not feel like requesting a spade shift. Had East played the three and then the ten of clubs, this would have asked for spades. West may therefore draw the inference that East likes diamonds and with this in mind, a shift to the king of diamonds can be considered.

You must be aware however, that nothing East has done can be construed as asking for a diamond shift. The only thing East has done is to deny the ability to ask for a spade shift. You shift to diamonds at your own risk.

This happens quite often. You may switch to one suit (usually clubs) when partner has not been able to request a switch to a higher ranking suit. Remember though that it is very seldom that partner can specify a switch to a lower ranking suit. The only message you may interpret from partner's cards in the above instance is "I cannot *call* for a higher ranking suit. You use your judgment."

Here are three more slightly unusual cases of suit preference at the first or second trick.

```
                North
                ♠ Q1073
                ♥ 93
                ♦ Q1087
West            ♣ K54          East       North    East     South    West
♠ 862                          ♠ 4        Pass     Pass     1♠       2♥
♥ AK7642                       ♥ QJ8       2♠       3♥       4♠       All Pass
♦ KJ53                         ♦ 62
♣ ———          South           ♣ Q987632
                ♠ AKJ95
                ♥ 105
                ♦ A94
                ♣ AJ10
```

West leads the heart king and East plays the queen, showing the jack as well. West then continues with the heart two to East's jack. East, realizing West would not overcall with only a four card suit, will recognize that West is calling for a club return. West will ruff it and eventually will score the diamond king for down one.

```
                North
                ♠ 93
                ♥ KJ9
                ♦ J1054
West            ♣ J1083        East       North    East     South    West
♠ AK1072                       ♠ QJ64     —        Pass     1♥       1♠
♥ 43                           ♥ Q2       2♥       2♠       4♥       All Pass
♦ AQ9                          ♦ 8762
♣ 942          South           ♣ 764
                ♠ 85
                ♥ A108765
                ♦ K3
                ♣ AKQ
```

This time, when East plays the queen on West's King, West continues with the spade ten! East should overtake the ten and return a diamond. Without this sequence of plays, declarer will make four hearts if he guesses the location of the heart queen.

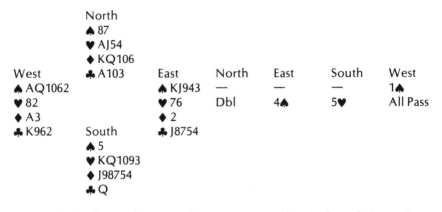

```
                North
                ♠ 87
                ♥ AJ54
                ♦ KQ106
West            ♣ A103      East       North    East    South    West
♠ AQ1062                    ♠ KJ943    —        —       —        1♠
♥ 82                        ♥ 76       Dbl      4♠      5♥       All Pass
♦ A3                        ♦ 2
♣ K962          South       ♣ J8754
                ♠ 5
                ♥ KQ1093
                ♦ J98754
                ♣ Q
```

West leads the spade ace and East must consider the best defense. From East's point of view, there will be no further spade trick (particularly if the partnership plays that an opening bid of one heart or one spade guarantees five). With this in mind, East would like West to play the ace and another diamond which East will trump. How can East tell West to do this? Only one card in East's hand will properly convey the message to West and that card is the king of spades! West will surely be surprised to see that card and hopefully will work out what it means. He should.

When West does cash the diamond ace, he may be a bit disappointed to see East's two, but the message of the king of spades is so unmistakably clear that West should have no problem continuing the suit. Down one again.

Suit Preferences During the Middle of the Hand

In some instances, it is possible to give partner some help in the defense during the later stages of the hand. This may be done by using a suit preference signal of some sort. A delayed suit preference can take a number of forms. It may be a wild out of the blue card. Or it may simply be a slightly unusual card played as part of a distributional count.

A card which is played while giving a distributional count can have suit preference overtones very much like the situation where one defender is giving a come on in a suit. The rule to remember is this:

If partner's card can be giving a come on or a count, then it is not a suit preference. It is the second card in such a series which can give a suit preference signal.

```
              North
              ♠ 96
              ♥ K9
              ♦ KQJ108
West          ♣ Q1098   East
♠ A10432                ♠ Q87        North    East     South    West
♥ 108                   ♥ A765       —        Pass     1♥       Pass
♦ A63                   ♦ 972        2♦       Pass     2NT      Pass
♣ 765         South     ♣ 432        3NT      All Pass
              ♠ KJ5
              ♥ QJ432
              ♦ 54
              ♣ AKJ
```

West's spade lead is taken by the king, East playing the queen. When dummy leads the king of diamonds, East plays the two to tell West how many diamonds he has, in this case three. West should play low on the first diamond. When declarer leads the queen of diamonds, East can play the nine to suggest a heart entry. West will know that:

1. East has three diamonds, or he would play the nine first to show he had only two.

2. East therefore did not have to play the nine on the second round of diamonds.

3. The nine of diamonds must be a suit preference signal. If West leads a heart to East's ace, the spade return will defeat three notrump.

Under no circumstances should West lead a club on the theory that East's first card was the deuce of diamonds. That card is clearly a count card showing how many diamonds East holds.

Once in a while when your holding in a suit is clearly known to partner, you can give a suit preference instead of a count. This is a rare occurrence which is much the exception to the normal rule. It might take some form like this one.

```
              North
              ♠ 2
              ♥ J
              ♦ KQJ9852
West          ♣ A654       East
♠ AKJ9                     ♠ 103        North    East    South    West
♥ Q7654                    ♥ 9832       —        —       1♠       Pass
♦ 1076                     ♦ A43        2♦       Pass    2♠       Pass
♣ 8           South        ♣ 10972      3♦       Pass    3NT      All Pass
              ♠ Q87654
              ♥ AK10
              ♦ ———
              ♣ KQJ3
```

The auction does not get any awards, but if the defense is sloppy, three notrump will make.

West leads a heart, taken by dummy's jack. Dummy next leads the diamond king. East will probably duck the first diamond. West now has the opportunity to make the unusual play of the diamond ten. This is safe because it cannot be misconstrued as a count signal. Declarer has shown out of diamonds on the first round, so the diamond count is known to both defenders. If West did not play the diamond ten on the first round, East might play low on the second diamond as well, hoping to persuade declarer to look elsewhere for tricks. This could be the case if South thought diamonds were four, two and therefore unestablishable due to lack of entries.

As you can see however, declarer needs only two tricks in diamonds to score three notrump. Only if East grabs the first or second diamond and leads a spade back will South be set.

The most spectacular instances of suit preference are quite rare, but when they occur they are quite impressive.

```
                 North
                 ♠ AKJ2
                 ♥ K7
                 ♦ Q754
West             ♣ Q65      East
♠ 109874                    ♠ Q5          North   East     South   West
♥ 432                       ♥ AQJ10       1♦      Pass     1♥      Pass
♦ J6                        ♦ 109832      1♠      Pass     2NT     Pass
♣ A43            South      ♣ 92          3NT     All Pass
                 ♠ 63
                 ♥ 9865
                 ♦ AK
                 ♣ KJ1087
```

South's choice of one heart does not help the defense any, but it can be
overcome. West leads the ten of spades, taken by the king. Next follows
three rounds of clubs, West taking the third, as East echoes to show two.
What should East discard on the third club? East cannot discard a heart, as all
the hearts are needed for tricks. A small diamond might work, but West
might merely continue spades. The one card East can play with safety is the
spade queen. It will be a very somnambulistic West who does not appreciate
this play! Result, down one.

The following is even more unusual.

```
                 North
                 ♠ AQ
                 ♥ J742
                 ♦ Q5
West             ♣ AKQ108   East
♠ 7654                      ♠ KJ102       North   East     South   West
♥ 9876                      ♥ A3          1♣      1♦       1NT     Pass
♦ A2                        ♦ K10876      3NT     All Pass
♣ 765            South      ♣ 32
                 ♠ 983
                 ♥ KQ10
                 ♦ J943
                 ♣ J94
```

West leads his partner's suit starting with the diamond ace. Dummy plays
the five and already the defense is at the crossroads. The only defense to set
three notrump is a spade switch now. If West continues diamonds, declarer
will make an overtrick without breathing hard.

How can East get a spade switch out of West? It is not easy, but it can be
done. East has to play the diamond king. East can count declarer's tricks and
it is clear that giving up a second diamond trick will not give declarer a fast

nine. If West shifts to a spade, declarer will fail by one trick. If West does not shift to a spade, East will be entitled to be a bit upset.

Be sure you realize that in both of the preceding hands the critical card used as a suit preference was clearly not a come on card nor was it giving count.

Suit Preferences — A Summary

At the risk of being repetitive, here are the considerations which must be applied to all suit preference signals.

When your partner plays a card, you may decide it is a suit preference signal. But before you decide that it is so, you must be sure that partner is not giving either a come on card or a count card. Only when it passes both tests can it be thought of as a suit preference card.

On the other side of the coin is the situation when you are trying to give a suit preference to your partner. You must remember that he will, or should, look at the card you play in terms of come on or count. Bear this in mind when you attempt a suit preference. If, in retrospect, the card you intend to play does not fit the definition for suit preference, then your partner will not, or should not, think it is. Rather, he will interpret it according to one of the other definitions.

If you find that the card you are considering will not work, then perhaps another one will. If you find that you have no card available which would be interpreted as suit preference, then perhaps you can find a sequence of cards which will convey your message.

If you find that there is no way to give a suit preference, do not try. Wishful thinking does not work in bridge, no matter how hard you try. Therefore do not try.

Proper application of the rules of suit preference signals will greatly increase the scope of your defensive play. Misuse of the same, however, will cause confusion and distrust in the partnership. It will not be worth it.

DEVYN PRESS INC.

3600 Chamberlain Lane, Suite 206, Louisville, KY 40241

1-800-274-2221

CALL TOLL FREE IN THE U.S. & CANADA
TO ORDER OR TO REQUEST OUR 64 PAGE
FULL COLOR CATALOG OF BRIDGE BOOKS,
SUPPLIES AND GIFTS.

Andersen THE LEBENSOHL CONVENTION COMPLETE
Baron THE BRIDGE PLAYER'S DICTIONARY
Blackwood COMPLETE BOOK OF OPENING LEADS
Boeder THINKING ABOUT IMPS
Bruno-Hardy 2 OVER 1 GAME FORCE: AN INTRODUCTION
Darvas & De V. Hart RIGHT THROUGH THE PACK
Grant
    BRIDGE BASICS 1: AN INTRODUCTION
    BRIDGE BASICS 2: COMPETITIVE BIDDING
    BRIDGE AT A GLANCE
    IMPROVING YOUR JUDGMENT: DOUBLES
Groner DUPLICATE BRIDGE DIRECTION
Hardy
    TWO-OVER-ONE GAME FORCE
    TWO-OVER-ONE GAME FORCE QUIZ BOOK
Harris BRIDGE DIRECTOR'S COMPANION (5th Edition)
Kay COMPLETE BOOK OF DUPLICATE BRIDGE
Kelsey THE TRICKY GAME
Lampert THE FUN WAY TO ADVANCED BRIDGE
Lawrence
    CARD COMBINATIONS
    COMPLETE BOOK ON BALANCING
    DYNAMIC DEFENSE
    HAND EVALUATION
    HOW TO READ YOUR OPPONENTS' CARDS
    JUDGMENT AT BRIDGE
    PARTNERSHIP UNDERSTANDINGS
    PLAY BRIDGE WITH MIKE LAWRENCE
    PLAY SWISS TEAMS WITH MIKE LAWRENCE
    WORKBOOK ON THE TWO OVER ONE SYSTEM
Lipkin INVITATION TO ANNIHILATION
Penick
    BEGINNING BRIDGE COMPLETE
    BEGINNING BRIDGE QUIZZES
Rosenkranz
    BRIDGE: THE BIDDER'S GAME
    TIPS FOR TOPS
    MORE TIPS FOR TOPS
    TRUMP LEADS
    OUR MAN GODFREY
Rosenkranz & Alder BID TO WIN, PLAY FOR PLEASURE
Rosenkranz & Truscott BIDDING ON TARGET
Simon
    WHY YOU LOSE AT BRIDGE
Thomas SHERLOCK HOLMES, BRIDGE DETECTIVE
Woolsey
    MATCHPOINTS
    MODERN DEFENSIVE SIGNALLING
    PARTNERSHIP DEFENSE
World Bridge Federation APPEALS COMMITTEE DECISIONS
    from the 1994 NEC WORLD CHAMPIONSHIPS

$11.95

ABOUT THE AUTHOR

Mike Lawrence's achievements at bridge continue to stagger the imagination. Although only in his early forties, he has amassed nearly fifteen thousand master points, which ranks him in the top twenty on the all-time ACBL list. His impressive list of victories at North America Bridge Championships includes the Vanderbilt, which he has won five times, the Reisinger in which he has four victories, the Men's teams which he has won twice, and the Spingold. Second place finishes include the Reisinger, the Vanderbilt, the Spingold three times, and four times in the Blue Ribbon Pairs. Add to these two World Championships (Stockholm 1970 and Taiwan 1971), two second places (Miami 1972 and Garuja, Brazil 1973), and a third place (Miami 1986), well over 100 Regional Championship wins, and many victories in lesser events.

Mike has become quite prolific bridge writer. His first bridge book, *How to Read Your Opponents' Cards* was named bridge book of the year in 1973 by Alfred Sheinwold. In 1976 Mike wrote *Judgment at Bridge* for which Sheinwold graciously created an introduction. Then followed *The Complete Book on Overcalls in Contract Bridge,* and similarly titled works on the topic of *Balancing* and *Hand Evaluation,* all of which Sheinwold has been pleased to introduce; *Overcalls* was Mike's second "bridge book of the year", taking Sheinwold's award for 1980. A digression from his role as an author-teacher is *True Bridge Humor,* and his book *Play a Swiss Team of Four With Mike Lawrence* has been described by many readers as equivalent to a novel, building suspense in such fashion that the reader couldn't put it down until it had been finished. Other recent efforts include *Dynamic Defense, Play Bridge With Mike Lawrence, False Cards, Card Combinations,* and pamphlets covering major suit raises, Jacoby Transfers, and Lebensohl.

Two decades ago Mike ventured to write in another of his fields of expertise; *Winning Backgammon* was published by Pinnacle in 1975. His most recent non-bridge creation is *Scrabble,* which was published by Bantam in 1987.

In addition to enjoying his writing, Mike is creative in other fields as well. His artistic bent has led him to the creation of ink abstracts, decoration of bottles in leather, and work in stained glass. He is also an avid collector of old comic books which he buys, sells and trades.

Mike's major efforts as a teacher has produced a series of week-long classes. He h traveled to several cities, set up residence for a week, and taught students of all experien levels. Comments from his students indicate that he is a most thorough and thoughtf instructor who is able to express himself logically, humorously, and in easily understan able terms.

Published by
Devyn Press, Inc.
Louisville, Kentucky

ISBN 0-910791-81-3

ISBN 0-910791-81-3
51195

PHOTO BY DIANE BARTON-PAINE